LARRY AND THE WEREWOLF

Jeff Goode

SAMANTHA,

THANK YOU SO MUCH
FOR BEING PART OF THE
DICK PISTON MYTHOLOGY

BROADWAY PLAY PUBLISHING INC
56 E 81st St., NY NY 10028-0202
212 772-8334 fax: 212 772-8358
BroadwayPlayPubl.com

"PROSTHESIS: MURDER
OVERNIGHT
SENSATIONS
ROANOKE JULY 17th
2010
(BUT JULY 16th was
even better)

LARRY AND THE WEREWOLF
© Copyright 2006 by Jeff Goode

First printing: October 2006
I S B N: 0-88145-318-8

Book design: Marie Donovan
Word processing: Microsoft Word
Typographic controls: Ventura Publisher
Typeface: Palatino
Printed and bound in the U S A

CONTENTS

ABOUT THE AUTHOR

Jeff Goode is an actor, director and screenwriter, and the author of over fifty plays, musicals and childrens shows.

A corn-fed Iowa youth, Jeff attended the University of Iowa, where he co-founded (with Todd Ristau and Stan Ruth) the original No Shame Theater (out of the back of a pickup truck), and began writing to feed his acting habit.

During his summers, Jeff traveled to Bar Harbor, Maine to help establish the Unusual Cabaret, and became the company's first resident playwright when the other playwrights missed their flights.

After graduating from two different colleges with degrees in everything but playwriting, Jeff moved to Chicago and wrote THE EIGHT: REINDEER MONOLOGUES and hasn't had a moment's peace since.

In 1997, Jeff came to Los Angeles to write the pilot for M T V's *Undressed*, and later created the animated series *American Dragon: Jake Long* for the Disney Channel.

You can follow Jeff's further adventures on his website: jeffgoode.com.

also published by Broadway Play Publishing Inc:
DRACULA RIDES AGAIN *and* MARLEY'S GHOST

LARRY AND THE WEREWOLF, Episodes 1-3, were first presented by Pantechnicon Artworks at the Bailiwick Directors Festival in Chicago on 3 October 1995. The cast and creative contributors were:

HARLEQUIN .... Jeff Goode
DICK PISTON .... Doug Steckel
ALFREDO CENTAURI .... Phil Gigante
SECOND CENTURION .... Shawn Douglass
THIRD CENTURION .... Eric A Pot
LARRY FINGERS .... Larrance Fingerhut
SPIKE .... Cheryl Snodgrass
THE WEREWOLF .... Sean Cooper
FANTASY DICK .... Dean Schmitt
FANTASY CHICK .... Jill Kraft
HELGA HERMOSA .... Inger Hatlen
CABAL .... Cheryl Graeff
BILL BOLA .... Shawn Douglass
BELLA BOLA .... Jennifer Shepard
BIEDERMANN .... Michael G Dowd
TODD MORTON .... Sean Cooper
HERBERTO HERMOSA .... Brad Light

Director .... Amy Lynn Pigott
Composer .... Larrance Fingerhut
Assistant director .... Margaret Dubé
Costumes .... Allison Gerlach
Lighting .... Richard Sobin
Technical director .... Eric A Pot

LARRY AND THE WEREWOLF, Episodes 4-21,
were first presented by the adobe theater company
(Christopher Roberts, Producer) at The Flea Theater
in New York in August 1998. The cast and creative
contributors were:

DICK PISTON . . . . Arthur Aulisi
FANTASY CHICK . . . . Stacey Leigh Ivey
FANTASY DICK . . . . Jim McCauley
LARRY FINGERS . . . . Michael Garin
SPIKE . . . . Janice O'Rourke
ALFREDO CENTAURI . . . . Vin Knight
MARCUS BENIGNUS . . . . Ian Helfer
GAIUS LUCIUS . . . . Derin Basden
HELGA HERMOSA . . . . Erin Quinn Purcell
HERBERTO HERMOSA . . . . Arthur Halpern
BIEDERMANN . . . . Jay Rosenbloom
CABAL . . . . Beau Ruland
BILL BOLA . . . . Jeremy Brisiel
BELLA BOLA . . . . Jacqui Malouf
SANISH GHOST . . . . Jay Reiss

Directors . . . . Jeremy Dobrish, Elyse Singer,
Michael Scheman & Gary Schwartz
Lighting design . . . . Paul Ziemer
Set design . . . . Matthew Maraffi
Costume design . . . . Meganne George
Sound design . . . . Chris Todd
Composer . . . . Michael Garin
Production manager . . . . Stephanie McCormick
Stage manager . . . . John Donahue
Assistant director . . . . Vanessa Edwards

Production assistant . . . . Liz Albertson
Production assistant . . . . Niamh McCormall
Postcard/photos . . . . Richie Fahey
Program illustrations . . . . Chris Marobella

DRAMATIS PERSONAE

DICK PISTON, *Hotel Detective*
FANTASY DICK, PISTON's *film noir fantasy*
FANTASY CHICK, PISTON's *film noir femme fatale*
LARRY FINGERS, *unassuming piano player and crimial mastermind*
SPIKE, *domanatrix lounge singer and double murderer*
TODD MORTON, *band manager*
HARLEQUIN, *macabre master of ceremonies*
MS CABAL, *corrupt hotel manager*
BILL BOLA, *bellboy, hitman, thug*
BELLA BOLA, BILL's *identical twin sister, disgraced Israeli assassin*
ALFREDO CENTAURI, *two thousand year-old Roman centurion*
MARCUS BENIGNUS, *second centurion*
GAIUS LUCIUS, *third centurion*
HELGA HERMOSA, *neurotic ingénue and night nurse*
HERBERTO HERMOSA, *the ghost of* HELGA's *husband*
WOLFGANG BIEDERMANN, *a very hairy man*
SANISH GHOST, *the* **real** *ghost of* HERBERTO HERMOSA

LARRY AND THE WEREWOLF is a murder-mystery serial comedy with gratuitous sex and violence and a cliffhanger ending every ten minutes.

Originally created as a late night series for Chicago's Pantechnicon Artworks, the script is written in ten-minute "episodes" which can be performed individually—as a featured segment in a larger sketch show—or bundled together to create LARRY AND THE WEREWOLF shows of any length: three episodes equal half-hour short, six episodes equals hour-long one-act, etc.

The play debuted in New York with adobe theater company, performed in weekly installments as a summer special event. It later ran at Portland's Theater Vertigo as a set of four one-acts. The play has been performed in its entirety as a Halloween marathon at Nebraska's Theater of the American West.

The versatile episodic structure makes LARRY AND THE WEREWOLF a show that is easily tailored to the unique production needs of any company.

my proverbial thanks to
Amy Lynn Pigott & Eric A Pot
and the Kitchen Workshop
to whom Dick Piston owes his life

LARRY
AND THE
WEREWOLF

EPISODE 1

"The story I'm gonna tell you, yer not gonna believe..."

CHARACTERS

HARLEQUIN
DICK PISTON
ALFREDO CENTAURI
SECOND CENTURION
THIRD CENTURION
LARRY FINGERS
SPIKE
THE WEREWOLF
FANTASY DICK
FANTASY CHICK
HELGA HERMOSA

HARLEQUIN

(Enter HARLEQUIN, *a macabre master of ceremonies.)*

HARLEQUIN: *(Sings:)* Come with me
on a moonlit night
and listen to
the howl of your imagination.
Awoo-oo.
Awoo-oo.

Come with me
on a moonlit day
and listen to
the werewolf's bay
Awoo-oo.
Awoo-oo.

Larry and the Werewolf
Larry and the Werewolf
LARRY AND THE WEREWOLF...

(Suddenly the dance is over.)

HARLEQUIN: Episode One!

DICK PISTON

PISTON: The story I'm gonna tell you, yer not gonna
believe. But every word of it is true. I know, because it
happened to me. My name is Dick Piston. Not the Dick
Piston from those erotic novels. The real one. Me. Dick
Piston, hotel detective. It all started one stormy night on
the windswept slopes of some god-forsaken mountain

just outside of Rome. The place was a little farming village called Athanos. The year was twelve B C.

ROME—TWELVE B C

(Sounds of a thunderstorm. Lightning flashes. Enter three rain-drenched Roman CENTURIONS.*)*

FIRST CENTURION: *(Shouting over the storm:)* Did you find him?

SECOND CENTURION: What?!

FIRST CENTURION: Did you find him?!

SECOND CENTURION: No!

FIRST CENTURION: What?!

SECOND CENTURION: No! *(Pause)* But we found this!

(The THIRD CENTURION *holds up a large gold crucifix. Lightning flashes. And they are all gone.)*

PISTON: But I guess before I start at the beginning, I should tell you about Larry Fingers...

LARRY'S DRESSING ROOM

*(*LARRY, *a harmless little man in a grey sweater, is sitting at the piano, noodling away. His lead singer* SPIKE *leans against the piano. She wears an eyepatch.)*

SPIKE: Do you ever wonder what it's all about, Larry? I mean, do you ever sit back and look at all this shit and think to yourself... What the hell is all this shit? I mean, what did I do to deserve this? I mean it's not like I ask for this shit. It just happens. Shit happens, Larry. Someone said that. Socrates or somebody. And it was a wise man who said that. Or if it was a woman, she was a wise woman. But I think it was Socrates.

(Pause. She looks at him, but he doesn't say anything.)

SPIKE: Do you think I'm beautiful, Larry? Don't answer
that. Never mind. I don't wanna know. Forget I
asked it... It's just... *(She looks at him.)* No, never mind,
I guess it doesn't matter. You don't hafta tell me. But
sometimes it's good to hear, y'know? Like sometimes
it's good to hear "I love you". But I don't expect anyone
to say they love me. Not after what I done. But I mean,
I guess that's what I mean, y'know what I mean? 'Cause
if you know what yer doin'—if ya got a purpose in life,
then it doesn't matter if you're pretty or talented or
funny. Or if you can fuck a man to death. None of
that matters. If I'm gonna be a star, Larry, if that's
my destiny, then I'm not gonna complain. But if I'm
gonna be workin' in this hole for the rest of my life...
(She quickly wipes away a tear.) Here I am talkin' your
ear off again. I must sound pretty stupid, huh, Larry?

*(LARRY places a jewelry box on the piano, and slides it
toward her.)*

SPIKE: What? For me? *(She opens the box. It contains a
large gold crucifix.)* Oh, Larry! It's beautiful! This will
go great with my costume. I'm gonna go put it on.
(She exits.)

*(LARRY lingers for a moment, noodling at the piano.
Enter the WEREWOLF.)*

WEREWOLF: Rrarh! *(It drops to its knees, pleading.)* RRarh!?

(No response from LARRY.)

WEREWOLF: *(Rising to its feet, points accusingly:)* GRrrrR...

(WEREWOLF exits. LARRY noodles.)

DICK PISTON'S OFFICE

PISTON: Let me tell you how Larry and the Werewolf first came into my life. It was a Friday night. Friday the 13th. I remember it like it was yesterday. Was there a full moon that night? I don't know. In my line of work, it seems like there's always a full moon. I'm Dick Piston, hotel detective. It was a slow night, so I was in my office working on the first chapter of my novel. It goes like this:

(PISTON *writes. As he talks,* FANTASY DICK *appears in his fantasy office.*)

PISTON: Chapter one. It was another lonely Friday night. On a Friday night in the city...

FANTASY DICK: On a Friday night in the city, the smoggy air chokes you like the stench of unrequited love. Or maybe that's the two bit stogies I've been smoking. I light another one anyway. If I'm lucky the cancer will take me before I decide to do it myself. I reach for the bottle in my desk and pour myself a double shot of denial. But I don't bother with the glass anymore. Just something else to clean. Like the smokey glass on my office door. With the dirty black stencil that spells "Dick Piston, Hotel Detective" if you're coming from the other side. From where I sit it spells "Failure". (*He takes another swig.*) I'm not religious, but I pray for a knock on that door.

(*Knock at the door*)

PISTON: And that's where it ends. I've been working on the first chapter of this novel for two years and I can never get past that knock on the door. Who's out there? ...I never find out. But that night. That Friday the 13th night with the moon hanging full in the sky. Or maybe not. Something happened. Something that had never happened before.

(Knock at the door, more insistent this time.)

PISTON: The door opened.

(The door to the fantasy office opens. The door to PISTON's *own office also opens.)*

PISTON: And a woman stepped inside.

(The FANTASY CHICK *enters* FANTASY DICK's *office, and* HELGA HERMOSA *staggers into* PISTON's *office.* HELGA *is covered in blood.* PISTON, *enthralled by the* FANTASY CHICK, *doesn't notice* HELGA, *and she staggers back out.)*

FANTASY DICK: She was all my teenage fantasies with five more years to ripen. I'd swear I never saw her before in my life, but she slinked into my heart like she knew the way. And when she leaned across my desk, and spoke my name...

FANTASY CHICK: Dick Piston...I need you.

FANTASY DICK: I hope you don't need change for the bus, 'cause you just melted everything in my pocket.

*(*HELGA *staggers back in.)*

FANTASY CHICK & HELGA: Help me.

*(*HELGA *collapses.* PISTON *notices her for the first time.)*

PISTON: OH!

(He tries to help her up, but she screams and collapses again.)

FANTASY CHICK: *(Gliding backward out of the room:)* Help me... Help me, Dick Piston, help me. Help me. Dick Piston, help me...

PISTON: *(Trying to help* HELGA:)* Are you all right?

FANTASY DICK: *(To* PISTON:)* Hey! Hey! She's getting away!

PISTON: Uh...get her room number—I mean, her phone number, or her name, get her name...

FANTASY CHICK: I need you...

PISTON & FANTASY DICK: Wait!

(But she is gone.)

HELGA: Murder!

PISTON: Have you been shot?!

HELGA: No.

PISTON: Stabbed?!

HELGA: No.

PISTON: Strangled?!

HELGA: No.

(Pause. PISTON's getting tired of guessing.)

PISTON: ...Beaten?

HELGA: How can you think of sex at a time like this, when there's a man lying dead in my suite with his lungs ripped out and his blood splattered all over the walls, the furniture, some of it on the ceiling? His fingers like they've been chewed off by a cat and his eyeballs gouged out of their sockets lying near him on the bed. And his intestines, or whatever these are called— *(She hands him an intestine.)*

PISTON: Ugh!

HELGA: Strewn about like—Waitaminute. Did I say his eyes were gouged out of their sockets? I meant his shoulders were gouged out of their sockets and lying near him on the bed—

PISTON: And this man, you say he was murdered?

HELGA: Oh my God, do you think so?

PISTON: Don't *you* think so?

HELGA: That would explain it. The lungs, the blood...

PISTON: What was this man doing in your suite?

HELGA: Decomposing.

PISTON: Yes, but how did he get into the room?

HELGA: He was already there when I arrived.

PISTON: He was?

HELGA: Do you think that matters?

PISTON: It may. Try to be as explicit as you can.

HELGA: Okay. *(Explicitly:)* My pale white hands gently grasp your turgid member, firmly but tenderly caressing the base of your penis with my tongue...

PISTON: *(Jumping back:)* YOW! The murder! Explicit about the murder!

HELGA: Oh. I was up in my room—

PISTON: What's the number?

HELGA: Suite 1017. And I heard someone call my name—

PISTON: And what is your name?

HELGA: Helga. Helga Hermosa.

PISTON: *(Lost in thought for a moment:)* Helga...Hermosa...

HELGA: What is it?

PISTON: I don't know. Your name... It's like...a creamy desert, and a fruity beverage.

HELGA: And your name. Dick Piston. Is like a powerful piece of greasy machinery. And part of a car. Oh my God, my jewelry! *(She runs out.)*

PISTON: Where are you going?

HELGA: My jewelry is still in the suite!

PISTON: The murderer could be in your suite!

(But she is gone. PISTON *calmly takes out his pistol and checks the chamber.)*

PISTON: *(Aside to the audience:)* Why did I let her go? Why didn't I try to stop her? Why am I standing here talking to you while Helga Hermosa rushes headlong into the proverbial jaws of the same fate that disembowelled the man in suite 1017? Maybe because I don't care. Maybe because a beautiful damsel in distress doesn't tug at my heart the way it does for some men. Maybe because I know the murderer isn't waiting for Helga Hermosa in her suite. Maybe because I know that he's standing right here. Thinking. Planning his next move. *(He thinks. He plans his next move.)* Or maybe it's because I have a key to the service elevator and I'll be in suite 1017 before Helga Hermosa reaches the lobby. *(He shows a set of keys—to the service elevator.)* Maybe she was never in any danger at all. *(He takes out his pistol again.)* Chapter two...

HELGA'S HOTEL ROOM

*(*PISTON *brandishes his pistol, searching the room for murderers.* HELGA *bursts in.* PISTON *turns his gun on her. She screams and puts up her hands.)*

HELGA: Dick Piston! You're the murderer??

PISTON: No, I took the service elevator. But good guess.

HELGA: My jewelry! *(She rushes over to a large jewelry box on the floor. She opens it. It is filled with expensive jewelry.)* No! *(She digs through it desperately, throwing jewelry everywhere.)* No, no, no. *(She has thrown all the jewelry on the floor.)* NOOO!

PISTON: Looks like they didn't take your jewelry.

HELGA: *(Suddenly calm:)* Yes. That's lucky.

PISTON: Where did you say you found the body?

HELGA: *(Pointing:)* There on the bed.

(While HELGA *begins groping the floor like she's looking for a lost contact lens,* PISTON *looks at the "bed" area, bends down as if to look under the bed.)*

PISTON: And there was blood?

HELGA: Everywhere. On the floor, on the ceiling, on the bed, the couch, the...whatever you call that thing in the corner.

PISTON: Helga. There isn't a body here.

HELGA: What!

PISTON: There's no body.

HELGA: But I'm telling you, he was right here on the bed.

PISTON: Helga, there is no body, no blood. And Helga, there's no bed. This is an unfurnished room.

HELGA: NOOO!

BLACKOUT

EPISODE 2

"People check in, but they don't check out..."

CHARACTERS

HARLEQUIN
HELGA HERMOSA
DICK PISTON
CABAL
BILL BOLA
BELLA BOLA
WOLFGANG BIEDERMANN
ALFREDO CENTAURI
LARRY FINGERS
SPIKE
TODD MORTON

HARLEQUIN

(HARLEQUIN, *chuckling to self slinks to center stage.*)

HARLEQUIN: LARRY AND THE WEREWOLF. Episode Two. *(Exiting:)* Awooooo...

HELGA'S HOTEL ROOM

HELGA: You have to believe me, Dick Piston, he was right here on the bed.

PISTON: Well, he's not here now. And neither is the bed.

HELGA: He's been kidnapped. Maybe there's a ransom note. *(She looks for a note.)*

PISTON: Helga, do you really think some one would kidnap a dismembered corpse?

HELGA: Do you have another explanation?

PISTON: Yes, I think I do.

HELGA: Tell me, tell me! If you can solve the murder, maybe it will lead us to the person who stole my jewelry. *(Catching herself:)* Oh no. My jewelry isn't missing. Never mind. Forget I mentioned it.

PISTON: You say you last saw this man here lying dead on the bed?

HELGA: Covered in bled.

PISTON: But he's not here now, which tends to suggest that the murderer is also a body snatcher.

HELGA: How diabolical!

PISTON: However the bed is also missing, along with everything else in the suite, the couch, the chairs—

HELGA: The thing in the corner.

PISTON: Everything except your jewelry.

HELGA: Thank God.

PISTON: Which tends to suggest that the murderer is also an interior decorator.

HELGA: *(Aghast:)* Oh, it's inhuman!

PISTON: However, the blood is also missing—

HELGA: That *is* strange.

PISTON: Blood which you describe as being splattered on the bed, the floor, the ceiling—

HELGA: The thing in the corner.

PISTON: But now there is not a drop of blood in evidence.

HELGA: Which tends to suggest that the murderer was also very absorbent!

PISTON: Um... Which tends to suggest that you, Helga, are a liar. Have a nice day.

HELGA: Where are you going?

PISTON: To my office, my work here is done.

HELGA: What about Herberto?

PISTON: Who is Herberto?

HELGA: That was his name.

PISTON: Oh, Herberto. Herberto...is a figment of your imagination.

HELGA: *Was* a figment.

PISTON: I'm sorry, Herberto *was* a figment of your imagination.

HELGA: What is he now?

PISTON: HE'S *STILL* A FIGMENT OF YOUR IMAGINATION! Herberto, as you choose to call him, is alive and well and living in a part of your subconscious that some people don't take with them to a hotel!!

HELGA: I see.

PISTON: If you need me, I'll be in my office. Please, don't hesitate to call. I assure you, this is the most excitement I've had in weeks.

HELGA: Mister Piston?

PISTON: Ms Hermosa?

HELGA: I know how this must look. I don't blame you if you don't want to help me. But I'm not crazy. Herberto is not an imaginary person. He's my husband.

PISTON: Herberto is your husband?

HELGA: This was supposed to be our honeymoon.

(The door opens and MS CABAL *the hotel manager comes in, flanked by* BILL *and* BELLA BOLA, *two thugs dressed as bellhops.)*

PISTON: Ms Cabal?

CABAL: *(Going to* HELGA:*)* Mrs Hermosa, I am very sorry to hear about your husband. I'm Ms Cabal, the hotel manager, if there's anything I or any of my staff can do to comfort you in your hour of need. Please let me know. Anything, really.

PISTON: You know about her husband?

CABAL: Well, yes. My staff informed me the moment it happened. Tragic really.

HELGA: He's not a figment of my imagination?

CABAL: Heavens, no. *(Aside to bellhops:)* Get this woman some gin, she's hysterical.

PISTON: Ms Cabal, when did you find out about the murder?

CABAL: What murder?

PISTON: Her husband's murder.

CABAL: Good God! Mister Hermosa wasn't murdered. He committed suicide.

HELGA: Suicide??

CABAL: Didn't you know? Oh God, I'm sorry, what a terrible way to find out.

PISTON: He committed suicide?

CABAL: Yes, he jumped from this very window. One of the bellhops found him a couple hours ago. See, there he is.

HELGA: *(Looking out the window:)* Oh, God, it's true!

CABAL: Now, now, Mrs Hermosa, you mustn't blame yourself.

HELGA: What! You think it's my fault?

CABAL: Well, you must have seen it coming. The debts. The depression. The drinking, the driving, the drugs! And then you threatened divorce! You practically drove him to it! Oh, here's a note he left at the front desk. If suicide is a cry for help, this man was yodeling.

HELGA: *(As she reads the note:)* Oh God, it's true!

CABAL: Now, now, Mrs Hermosa, you mustn't blame yourself.

PISTON: Can I talk to you, Ms Cabal?

CABAL: Yes, Piston, what is it?

PISTON: *(Taking* CABAL *aside:)* Have the police been here yet?

CABAL: Not yet.

PISTON: Is that how the body was found?

CABAL: I think so, yes. Hey, kid, get away from there! That's not a toy! Stupid kid.

PISTON: There's something suspicious about this suicide.

CABAL: What is it, Piston?

PISTON: Well, it looks to me like Mister Hermosa tore out his own throat before hurling himself from this window.

CABAL: *(Nervous:)* Hmm.

PISTON: And are those his arms?

CABAL: They could be his.

PISTON: *(With determination:)* This wasn't a suicide. Let me see that note.

(PISTON reaches for the note, but CABAL snatches it away.)

CABAL: All right, I did it!

PISTON & HELGA: What!

CABAL: I threw him out the window.

HELGA: You killed my husband?

CABAL: Don't be ridiculous. He was dead when I got here. But me and the bellboys cleaned the place up and tried to make it look like a suicide.

PISTON: What about the furniture?

CABAL: We're having it cleaned.

PISTON: Why??

CABAL: To preserve the reputation of this hotel, Piston. You should know that. We can't have a bizarre murder here. It's scandalous! We'd be ruined.

PISTON: And a bizarre suicide isn't scandalous?

CABAL: Of course not. Happens all the time. People check in, but they don't check out. Why die in the squalid desolation of your own home, when you can come to the Lakeview Hotel and leave life in luxury. It's like a service we provide. But a grisly murder with the killer still at large. That's different. Makes the other guests edgy. "Who did it?" "Who's next?" "What was that sound?" We can't have that. We want our guests to be comfortable. Especially on their honeymoon. So, if there's anything you need Mrs Hermosa...

PISTON: We have to report this to the police.

CABAL: No. No police. I mean it, Piston.

PISTON: This is insane.

CABAL: It may be insane, but I sleep with the person who signs your paychecks, so until you make the best seller lists, you better think twice about crossing me, Piston. No police.

PISTON: But the murderer's still at large.

CABAL: And the less said about it, the better.

PISTON: But what if he strikes again? Won't that make your guests nervous?

CABAL: Good point. Hmmm. All right. You've got twenty minutes. If you can solve this case before I get back from the masseuse, good. If not, we're gonna have to go with the self-inflicted vivisection story.

PISTON: The police will never buy that.

CABAL: Ho ho, you let me worry about the police and what they will buy. You just find this psycho and get him or her out of my hotel before the other guests get wind of it. I don't want a panic on my hands. Very sorry about your husband, Mrs Hermosa.

(CABAL *exits. The bellhops enter with a big, weird thing.*)

BELLHOP: Here's your thing.

HELGA: Oh, that goes in the corner.

DICK PISTON

PISTON: Why didn't I go to the police? Well... All right, I shoulda gone to the police! But if I *had* gone to the police, Cabal's bellhops would have been all over the scene in no time. She was right about the suicides. Every week, two or three pathetic losers or successful rock stars would off themselves in one of the cheap rooms, and the hotel staff had become quite expert at sanitizing a death suite—as we call them in the business. My only chance to get at the clues in this case was to go along with Cabal's crazy scheme for now. I told you you wouldn't believe it. I wouldn't believe it myself, except I was there. Me. Dick Piston, hotel detective. But enough about me, let me tell you about the suspects...

BIEDERMANN'S ROOM

PISTON: My first stop was room 1016—the suite adjoining room 1017 on the south. Through this door, the murderer could have entered the Hermosa suite unobserved by the hotel staff or other patrons in the hallway.

BIEDERMANN: *(Offstage:)* What?

PISTON: The room was registered to a Mister Wolfgang Biedermann.

BIEDERMANN: *(Offstage:)* Is there someone out there?

PISTON: Mister Biedermann?

BIEDERMANN: *(Offstage:)* Who is it?

PISTON: Dick Piston, hotel detective. I'd like to ask you a few questions.

BIEDERMANN: *(Offstage:)* Come on in, detective, I'm in the bathroom.

PISTON: *(Uneasy:)* I can come back, if you're...if you're...

BIEDERMANN: *(Offstage:)* Taking a dump? No, I'll be at it a couple of hours, so you better ask me now.

PISTON: A couple of hours?

BIEDERMANN: *(Offstage:)* Yeah. I have a colon disorder. Colonic loctitus. Makes bowel movements very, um, laborious.

PISTON: Ew.

BIEDERMANN: *(Offstage:)* It's not painful, but it sure puts the toil in the word toilet.

PISTON: Oh.

BIEDERMANN: *(Offstage:)* Don't worry though, it's not contagious. Here, take a look at this.

(BIEDERMANN *hands* PISTON *some photos.)*

PISTON: *(Looking at them:)* WO!! What the hell is that?

BIEDERMANN: *(Offstage:)* That's my rectum. Doctor gave me those. Costs more for color, but I think it's worth it, don't you?

PISTON: *(Thrashing about:)* OH MY GOD.

BIEDERMANN: *(Offstage:)* See that yellowish rash?

PISTON: I'm gonna throw up!

BIEDERMANN: *(Shutting the door:)* Occupied!

(PISTON *rushes out of the room.)*

HARLEQUIN

HARLEQUIN: I want to be fictional. I want to come alive in your imagination. And live there. And die. And then live again in your dreams, your fantasies, your delusions. I want to be free from trouble. Even in the darkest tragedy never to be trapped in a dilemma. Because no matter what the catastrophe, it ends on the final page. ...Not like this. *(Exiting:)* Not like this...

OUTSIDE SUITE 1018

PISTON: Suite 1018 adjoins the Hermosa suite on the north. I still have questions for Mister Biedermann, but I want to give my stomach a chance to settle.

(PISTON knocks at the door. Door opens. It is the First Centurion from 12 B C, but in modern dress.)

ALFREDO: Yes?

PISTON: I'm Dick Piston, hotel detective.

ALFREDO: Alfredo Centauri.

PISTON: Can I ask you a couple questions, Mister Centauri?

ALFREDO: What does it pertain to, Mister Piston?

PISTON: I'm afraid there's been a murder in the hotel.

ALFREDO: Ah, yes, in the adjoining suite.

PISTON: How did you know?

ALFREDO: I hear the screams.

PISTON: You heard the screams?! About two hours ago?

ALFREDO: Just now. Not the victim. I hear the woman's screams. Helga. She cries for him.

(HELGA's *weeping can be heard faintly.*)

ALFREDO: The victim was...her lover?

PISTON: Her husband, Herberto Hermosa.

ALFREDO: Ah. How was he killed? Violently?

PISTON: He was mauled to death, and his internal organs, arms and throat ripped out.

ALFREDO: So, yes, violently.

PISTON: Yes.

ALFREDO: And you have questions for me?

PISTON: Just a few. Did you know the Hermosas, Mister Centauri?

ALFREDO: Alfredo.

PISTON: Alfredo. ...Did you?

(*Pause*)

ALFREDO: I am afraid I cannot be of help to you, Mister Piston, and I am very busy right now. But if this man was murdered in the way you describe... I would suggest you talk to Larry Fingers.

PISTON: Larry Fingers? The musician?

ALFREDO: Larry Fingers.

(ALFREDO *starts to leave.*)

PISTON: (*Putting his hand on* ALFREDO's *shoulder:*) Waitaminute.

ALFREDO: (*Removing* PISTON's *hand with a deft, but painful wrist hold:*) Not now, Mister Piston. Larry Fingers has the answers you seek. Goodbye.

(ALFREDO's *door closes.*)

PISTON: (*Placing a call on a cellular phone:*) Ms Cabal, this is Dick Piston. Tell your bellhops to make sure Mister

Centauri doesn't leave the hotel. I'm going to have a talk with Larry Fingers.

THE HOTEL STAGE

(LARRY's *manager introduces the band:*)

TODD: *(Voice over:)* Ladies and Gentlemen, the Lakeview Hotel is proud to present: Larry Fingers! And Spike!!

(SPIKE *is in her leather rock and roll outfit. She wears the crucifix prominently. She is not wearing her eyepatch.*)

SPIKE: *(Sings seductively, teasing:)*
If I were a secret, would you want to know?
If I were a party, would you want to go?
There's a fantasy inside of me,
and maybe...
just maybe...
you're not invited.

If I were a journey, would you try to make it?
If I were a cake, do you think you could take it?
There's a fantasy inside of me,
and maybe...
just maybe...
you're not invited.
(Suddenly changing tempo, she sings dangerously:)
Billie was a girl with a past
said the past was a blast
but she knew it couldn't last
movin' way too fast
...for a girl with a past.

Billy was a boy on the run
on the run with a gun
said what's done is done

havin' too much fun
...for a boy with a gun

Billie was afraid, was alone
Billy took her home
He wouldn't let her use the phone
Till he made her his own.
Hey, Billy, leave that girl alone!

(Gunshots or explosions or a drum solo)

SPIKE: Billie is a girl with a past
on the run with a gun
havin' too much fun
and she knew it wouldn't last
but what's done is done
movin' way too fast
...for a girl with a past.

You don't judge a book by the gloss of its cover.
So don't look too deep when you look at your lover.
There's a fantasy inside of me,
and maybe...
just maybe...
you are invited.

TODD: That was beautiful, Larry, beautiful.

SPIKE: *(Exiting:)* Shut up, Todd.

TODD: *(Following her out:)* Beautiful, Spike, beautiful.

PISTON: *(Appearing out of the shadows:)* Larry Fingers?
I'm Dick Piston, hotel detective. I'm investigating a
murder up on the tenth floor, and your name came up.
It seems that one of my suspects thinks you might be
able to shed some light on this case. He said that if a
man has been torn to shreds in his own room, Larry
Fingers is the man to talk to. Why do you think he said
that, Larry? Did he see you up there?

(SPIKE reenters.)

SPIKE: Who are you?

PISTON: I'm the hotel detective. I'm investigating a murder.

SPIKE: Oh. How can we help you, detective?

PISTON: Well, for starters, you could tell me where you both were two hours ago.

SPIKE: You think *we* did it?

PISTON: I'm just trying to be thorough.

SPIKE: Why would we be on the tenth floor? Our rooms are right off the stage in the main ballroom.

PISTON: That may be, Miss, but Mister Fingers has been implicated in this case by one of the neighbors.

SPIKE: Somebody fingered Larry?

PISTON: Alfredo Centauri.

SPIKE: Never heard of him.

PISTON: Larry?

SPIKE: And Larry's never heard of him either! You ought to take another look at your Alfredo Centauri.

PISTON: Oh, I will. *(To* LARRY:*)* How about Herberto Hermosa, you ever heard of him?

SPIKE: I have. He's the guy who jumped out of his window.

PISTON: Mister Hermosa didn't jump. He was pushed.

SPIKE: The manager told us it was suicide.

PISTON: Yes, that's the official story. But if you take a look at the body, you'll see that Mister Hermosa was attacked by a bear on the way down.

SPIKE: So you're looking for a flying bear?

PISTON: I'm looking for a murderer!

SPIKE: And you think it's Larry? Look at him. Larry's no killer. This is the kindest, gentlest man alive.

PISTON: George Bush's America was kind and gentle, but I wouldn't leave it alone in a room with an Iraqi army.

SPIKE: What are you saying?

PISTON: Nothing, Spike. But I've been on this case for ten minutes and so far it's been nothing but dead ends and closed doors.

SPIKE: Well, you've run into another one, detective, because two hours ago, Larry was with me. On stage. Playing the piano. Now, if there's nothing further. We'd both appreciate it if you'd leave us alone. We've got a show to do. *(Exiting:)* Larry, I'll be in the sauna.

PISTON: I'm sorry to trouble you, Mister Fingers. I'll be going now. But there's still one question maybe you can answer. If you're not involved, why would Alfredo Centauri give me your name? *(Pause.* LARRY *places a box on the piano and exits.* PISTON *opens the box and looks inside.)*

PISTON: Silver bullets?

DICK PISTON

PISTON: There are three ways to kill a werewolf. Wolfsbane. Nuclear weapons. And silver bullets. But I'm getting way ahead of myself. You see, I didn't suspect lycanthropy was involved until after I'd questioned Helga Hermosa.

HELGA'S ROOM

(HELGA *is trying to open a twist-off bottle, when she sees* PISTON.)

HELGA: Mister Piston? What are you doing here?

PISTON: I'd like to ask you a few questions.

HELGA: Oh my God, am I a suspect?? You think I killed my husband???

PISTON: No, not at all. Well, I mean, yes, everybody's a suspect, but no I don't think... What would be your motive?

HELGA: I don't know.

PISTON: And the strength it would take to wrench his arms out of their sockets, would be...would be... (*Watches her struggling with the bottle:*) Actually, I don't know anyone who could have committed this crime, so if you don't mind, I have a few of routine questions.

HELGA: Okay.

PISTON: Did your husband have any enemies?

HELGA: Do you mean natural enemies like wolves and mountain lions, or do you mean foreign countries he was at war with?

PISTON: Um, no, I mean, like, people who might want to kill him.

HELGA: Oh, I don't think so. Maybe. Put maybe.

PISTON: Did your husband drink?

HELGA: Like a fish.

PISTON: I see.

(HELGA *makes fish faces.*)

HELGA: Like that.

PISTON: Excuse me?

HELGA: That's how he would drink. *(Makes fish face again.)* Like a fish. He did it just to irritate me. Ooh, I hated that! I just wanted to...to... *(Tries to think of another word for "dismember", can't think of one.)* Argh!! *(She pops the bottle open.)*

PISTON: *(A little bit stunned:)* Sounds like the honeymoon was over.

HELGA: *(Cheerful again:)* Oh God, yes, I only married him for the money.

(Dead silence)

PISTON: Helga?

HELGA: Yes?

PISTON: Where were you at the time of the murder?

HELGA: Where was...? Oh, I see what you're thinking. Honestly, Mister Piston, I'm not your man. I have an airtight alibi.

PISTON: You do?

HELGA: Sure.

PISTON: What is it?

HELGA: I can't tell you.

PISTON: You can't tell me?

HELGA: It's a secret.

PISTON: Ms Hermosa, if you can't tell me what your airtight alibi is, then you don't have one.

HELGA: Uh oh.

PISTON: Where were you at the time of the murder?

HELGA: Um...

PISTON: WHERE WERE YOU?!

HELGA: I was with my lover! There, are you satisfied?

PISTON: Your lover? Who is he? What's his name?

HELGA: No!

PISTON: Tell me his name!

HELGA: I don't want him involved!

PISTON: This isn't a game, Helga. There's something very peculiar going on at this hotel, and I'm going to get to the bottom of it!

HELGA: No, please, no! It would ruin him if people found out.

PISTON: *(Grimly drawing his gun and pointing it at her:)* Tell me his name.

HELGA: It's you.

BLACKOUT

EPISODE 3

"Come on, do I look like a werewolf to you?"

CHARACTERS

HARLEQUIN
HELGA HERMOSA
DICK PISTON
ALFREDO CENTAURI
CABAL
BILL BOLA
BELLA BOLA
LARRY FINGERS
SPIKE
WOLFGANG BIEDERMANN
FANTASY CHICK
FANTASY DICK
HERBERTO HERMOSA

HARLEQUIN

HARLEQUIN: LARRY AND THE WEREWOLF. Episode Three. Awooooo... *(Disappears)*

HELGA'S HOTEL ROOM

HELGA: It's you! You're the murderer!

(HELGA *takes advantage of* PISTON'S *surprise to bite his wrist and snatch his gun away.*)

HELGA: You killed my husband, and now you were going to kill me so there won't be any witnesses. Oh, it's all becoming perfectly clear. There is no service elevator. You were here in this room the whole time, and that was some sort of hologram I talked to in your office. You shot my husband, then you ripped his guts out to recover the incriminating evidence. The bullets. Which any ballistics expert could match with the bullets in this gun—the murder weapon! *(She looks in the gun.)* Silver bullets?

(PISTON *takes advantage of* HELGA'S *distraction to grab her arm.* HELGA *struggles, but he very easily throws her to the ground and recovers his weapon.*)

HELGA: Now what are you going to do? Shoot me in the head and then decapitate me and have my skull teleported to your spaceship?

PISTON: You are a wacko.

HELGA: You had motive. You had opportunity. You have the strength of ten men.

PISTON: I DON'T HAVE THE STRENGTH OF TEN MEN! But I think I know who does.

(He starts to leave.)

HELGA: Wait, I'm coming with you!

PISTON: Maybe in the movie version. *(He leaves without her.)*

(ALFREDO appears from behind a plant. HELGA doesn't see him. She leaves.)

THE INFINITE CENTURION

ALFREDO: Justice is a scalpel.
It cuts through skin and flesh and bone to get at the heart of the truth.

No. Justice is a dagger.
It knows nothing of anatomy.
It plunges at random into the body.
It knows only that the heart is somewhere inside.

No. Justice is the heart.
It knows nothing.
Only a feeling when the truth is near.

And the truth is a dagger.

HELGA'S HOTEL ROOM

(PISTON answers a knock at the door. It's CABAL with two of the bellhops.)

CABAL: What the hell is going on here, Piston?

PISTON: Just a gathering of the usual suspects. Thank you for coming.

CABAL: Everyone in the hotel is talking murder. I told you not to go public with this thing. *(To the bellhops:)* Bill, Bella, beat the crap out of this dick.

(The bellhops beat the crap out of PISTON. HELGA *enters.)*

HELGA: Miss Cabal!

CABAL: Mrs Hermosa, are you enjoying your stay at our hotel?

HELGA: Oh, yes, it's been quite lovely since my husband died.

CABAL: Excellent.

HELGA: What are they doing to Mister Piston?

CABAL: Oh, he was choking on some food.

(The bellhops stop beating PISTON.)

CABAL: Piston, can you breathe yet?

(PISTON *wheezes.)*

CABAL: Nope, better keep at it.

(Bellhops resume punching PISTON *in the stomach. A knock at the door)*

CABAL: Hold it.

(They stop beating him up. HELGA *opens the door. It's* LARRY *and* SPIKE.)

CABAL: Larry Fingers! What are you doing here?

PISTON: I invited him. Come in, Larry.

HELGA: *(Screams:)* AAH! Larry Fingers! It's Larry Fingers! I love you, Larry. I have all your music.

SPIKE: *(Entering:)* Back off, blondie. Larry doesn't like to be touched.

CABAL: What is this, Piston?

PISTON: I thought it would be nice to invite everyone back to the scene of the crime.

SPIKE: I told you, Piston, Larry was with me at the time of the murder.

PISTON: Yes, you said that, Spike. On stage. But I've seen your act and Larry stands *behind* you and to the right. That's your glass eye, isn't it? So you didn't actually *see* Larry at all, did you?

SPIKE: I don't have to see him. He plays the keyboard. I can hear him.

PISTON: Ah, yes, but isn't it one of those fancy state-of-the-art keyboards that lets you record a song and play it back later at the touch of a button? How do you know Larry didn't hit replay and slip off to commit a heinous murder during your opening number?

SPIKE: Because... Because...Larry?

PISTON: Larry himself gave me the clue which helped break this case. *(Holds up his gun:)* Silver bullets.

CABAL: My God, the Lone Ranger's calling card!

PISTON: ...Yes, but it's also one of the three ways to kill a werewolf.

HELGA: My husband was a werewolf?!

PISTON: Would you people shut up and let me solve this case!?!

HELGA & CABAL: Sorry.

PISTON: Your husband was killed by a werewolf. Only a hideous supernatural beast would have the strength to wrench a man's limbs from his torso.

(BILL raises his hand. BELLA elbows him, and he puts it back down.)

PISTON: But you knew that, didn't you, Larry?

(Everyone looks at LARRY. *He is silent.)*

CABAL: Get him!

(Bellhops start toward LARRY, *but* PISTON *stops them.)*

PISTON: But Larry Fingers is not the murderer. He knew about the werewolf. But he was on stage at the time of the murder.

SPIKE: But you said—

PISTON: Anything to shut you up. *(Continuing:)* There's one other person in this hotel who knew the murderer was a lycanthrope.

(They all look at each other.)

PISTON: The man who gave me Larry's name. The man in the adjoining suite. Alfredo Centauri. *(He throws open the door to the adjoining suite.)* Could you come in here, please, Mister Centauri? *(Nothing happens.)* Mister Centauri?

CABAL: He's gone.

PISTON: What?

CABAL: He checked out a few minutes ago.

PISTON: But I told you not to let him leave the hotel!

CABAL: Yes. But Mister Centauri told me something you could not have known at the time.

EVERYBODY: What?

CABAL: He told me *he* was the murderer.

(Everybody gasps.)

PISTON: AND YOU LET HIM GO???

CABAL: I don't have your warped sense of "values", Piston. I wanted the murderer *out* of the hotel, and Alfredo Centauri gave me the opportunity to do that without police involvement. He confessed to the crime so I let him pay his bill and go.

(Everybody murmurs.)

PISTON: But Alfredo Centauri isn't the werewolf, you idiot! He only said that so you'd let him leave. He's hiding something, though. But the real murderer is still in this building.

HELGA: Who is it??

PISTON: The final piece of the puzzle was also the first clue to fall into my proverbial lap.

EVERYBODY: What? What?

PISTON: *(Taking out the* BIEDERMANN *photo:)* This photo!

EVERYBODY: *(Thrashing about:)* OH MY GOD.

PISTON: *(Triumphantly:)* That is no human rectum.

SPIKE: How awful!

HELGA: It's like the inside of some hideous supernatural beast!

PISTON: And the colon in that photo belongs to Wolfgang Biedermann! The man in the other adjoining suite!

CABAL: Get him!

(The bellhops rush out.)

PISTON: *(Calling after them:)* Check in the toilet!

(Sound of a struggle in the next room.)

BIEDERMANN: *(Offstage:)* No! No! I'm innocent! Innocent, I tell you!

(Enter the bellhops with BIEDERMANN—*obviously a werewolf.)*

BIEDERMANN: *(Growls:)* What's everybody staring at? Come on, do I look like a murderer to you? I'm just here on vacation.

PISTON: *(Drawing his gun:)* It won't wash, Wolfgang.

BIEDERMANN: I'm not a werewolf. You gotta believe me. I wouldn't hurt a flea. *(He scratches behind his ear.)*

HELGA: You beast! You monster! You killed my husband!

SPIKE: And you're ugly.

BIEDERMANN: *(Lunging at* SPIKE:) Yaargh!

(The bellhops grab his arms, but BIEDERMANN *throws them off.* PISTON *shoots* BIEDERMANN *five or six times and he falls dead. Lights fade on the scene.)*

CABAL: Good work, Piston...

IN THE DARKNESS

FANTASY CHICK: I need you...Dick Piston.

(Lights come up on the Fantasy Office. FANTASY DICK *and the* FANTASY CHICK, *very close.)*

FANTASY DICK: Part of me wants to believe you. But it's not the part that pays the bills.

(The real PISTON *is also discovered, writing feverishly.* FANTASY CHICK *looks in her purse.)*

FANTASY CHICK: I see I'm going to have to give you a little incentive.

FANTASY DICK: In my line of work it's called a retainer.

*(FANTASY CHICK *takes a condom out of her purse.)*

FANTASY CHICK: In my line of work it's called a little incentive.

(She is about to kiss him. Suddenly a werewolf leaps in through the window.)

BIEDERMANN: Rrargh!!

*(*FANTASY DICK *and the* FANTASY CHICK *scream and run away. The werewolf chuckles.)*

PISTON: *(Putting down his pencil:)* It's no use. Ever since that night, I can't stop thinking about werewolves. I can't write without writing about werewolves. I can't sleep without dreaming about werewolves—

BIEDERMANN: Whoa whoa whoa! Hold on there, detective. I'm not a dream. I'm a ghost come back to haunt you. I usually show up in your dreams because... well, hell, you've got *great* dreams! I mean, who is this chick? She's hot! That dream last night with you and her and the dishwasher and the panda... Why can't you write something like that? I'd buy a copy.

PISTON: *(Through gritted teeth:)* I'm trying to.

BIEDERMANN: *(Coyly:)* I'm sorry, am I distracting you? Well, I guess that's what haunting is about. *(Haunting him:)* Wooo! Haunt, haunt!

(Another ghost climbs in through the window.)

HERMOSA: Hey, can I haunt him, too?

BIEDERMANN: Sure, come on up.

PISTON: Who the hell are you?

HERMOSA: I'm Herberto Hermosa, nice to meet you. Wooo...

PISTON: What do you want to haunt me for?

HERMOSA: You let my killer go free.

PISTON: *(Fed up:)* There's your killer, right there!!

*(*HERMOSA *squints at* BIEDERMANN.)*

HERMOSA: No. That's not him. I was killed by a werewolf.

PISTON: HE IS A WEREWOLF!!!

BIEDERMANN: There you go again. I told you, I'm not a werewolf.

BIEDERMANN & HERMOSA: *(Haunting:)* Wooo...

PISTON: Leave me alone!

HERMOSA: Sorry, we're gonna haunt you until you bring the real murderer to justice. Wooo...

PISTON: I did!!! Shut up, you stupid ghosts!

(The phone rings.)

BIEDERMANN: You better get that.

(They stop haunting. PISTON glares at them. They wait for him to get the phone.)

PISTON: *(On the phone:)* Hello?

HERMOSA: *(To BIEDERMANN:)* Hey, let me see if I can channel this guy! *(He concentrates.)* Let's see, he says: "This is the coroner's office. We finished the autopsy on Biedermann."

PISTON & BIEDERMANN: Uh huh.

HERMOSA: Um, "everything checks out with your story", yadda yadda yadda, something about self defense.

BIEDERMANN: That is amazing! How do you do that?

HERMOSA: "One question though. Seems like a typo on your statement here. Says you shot him with silver bullets."

PISTON: Uh huh.

HERMOSA: "But the slugs we removed from Biedermann were ordinary lead."

PISTON: What!

BIEDERMANN: I knew it!

HERMOSA: "It's okay, we're just gonna make the change to your statement, but you'll need to come in on Monday and sign it again."

(PISTON is in shock.)

HERMOSA: Ta da!

BIEDERMANN: *(To HERMOSA:)* That was great!

(PISTON hangs up the phone.)

BIEDERMANN: *(Starts to haunt:)* Wooo...

HERMOSA: *(Stopping him:)* Not now. Give him a minute to think.

(They fade away. PISTON looks at the bullets in his gun.)

PISTON: Somebody switched the bullets in my gun. Biedermann wasn't a werewolf at all. Just a hairy man with colonic loctitus and a bad smoker's cough. I murdered an innocent man. *(Beat)* And the real werewolf is still out there...

BLACKOUT

CURTAIN CALL

EVERYBODY: Join us again
when the moon is bright
to listen to
the howl of your imagination.

Join us here
when the moon is dark
and the werewolf's bite
is worse than its bark.

Awoo-oo!
Awoo-oo!

Larry and the Werewolf.
Larry and the Werewolf.
Larry and the Werewolf!

AWOO!!

THE
DEATH OF
DICK
PISTON

EPISODE 4

"Are there any other mysterious goings-on I should
know about?"

CHARACTERS

HARLEQUIN
BILL BOLA
BELLA BOLA
DICK PISTON
ALFREDO CENTAURI
SECOND CENTURION
THIRD CENTURION

HARLEQUIN

HARLEQUIN: LARRY AND THE WEREWOLF. Episode Four! Awooooo...

HELGA HERMOSA'S HOTEL ROOM

(BILL *and* BELLA, *the bellhops, are dusting.*)

BELLA: *(As she dusts:)* What's your name?

BILL: Bill.

BELLA: What's your last name?

BILL: Bola.

BELLA: What's your full name?

BILL: Bill Bola.

BELLA: What do you do?

BILL: Kill...oop.

BELLA: Caught you again.

(BILL *gives her a dollar. They go back to dusting.*)

BELLA: What's my name?

BILL: Bill...Bella! Your name is Bella!

BELLA: You said, "Bill" first.

BILL: No fair.

(*He gives her a dollar.*)

BELLA: What's your name?

BILL: Bill.

BELLA: What's your last name?

BILL: Bola.

BELLA: What do you do?

BILL: Bellboy.

BELLA: We received an anonymous tip....

BILL: I just work here.

(BELLA stops dusting.)

BELLA: Very good!

BILL: I practiced.

BELLA: I can tell.

(She gives him a dollar.)

BILL: *(To himself:)* What's my name, Bill, what do I do, bellboy...

(PISTON bursts in, weapon in hand. BILL and BELLA stop dusting.)

PISTON: What are you doing?

BILL: Don't tell me.

BELLA: We're dusting for fingerprints. What's it look like?

PISTON: That's not how you dust for fingerprints.

BELLA: Do you see any fingerprints?

PISTON: Well, stop it.

BELLA: Why?

PISTON: Somebody in this room switched the bullets in my gun.

(BILL and BELLA exchanges glances. Suddenly...)

BELLA: *(Pointing at BILL:)* It was him! I saw him do it!

PISTON & BILL: What?

(While PISTON *is distracted,* BELLA *disarms him and takes his gun.)*

BELLA: *(Turning the gun on* PISTON, *and edging toward the door:)* All right, Piston, I don't know how you figured out it was us, but Bill and me's walkin' out of here, see? I don't know why my little brother switched your bullets, but you gotta believe me, we didn't kill Hermosa.

BILL: I didn't switch the bullets.

BELLA: Yes, you did.

BILL: No, I didn't.

BELLA: Then who did?

BILL: I thought you did it.

BELLA: Why would I do it?

BILL: I dunno.

BELLA: Well, somebody in this room switched the bullets!

BILL: *(Suddenly pointing at* PISTON:*)* It must be him!

BELLA: All right, Piston, why'd you switch the bullets in your gun?

PISTON: I didn't.

BELLA: *(Turning to* BILL *again:)* So it *was* you?

BILL: I just work here.

PISTON: *(Snatching the gun away from* BELLA, *irritably:)* Somebody in this room—*earlier today when there were all those people in this room*—switched the bullets in my gun.

BILL & BELLA: Oh.

PISTON: Have you seen Helga?

BELLA: She checked out.

PISTON: I knew it! She must be the werewolf. You two, tell Cabal. I'm going to find Larry Fingers. He might be her next victim.

(PISTON *leaves.*)

BELLA: He checked out, too.

(PISTON *comes back.*)

PISTON: What?

BELLA: Larry Fingers checked out.

PISTON: *(Thinking:)* So maybe *he's* the werewolf....

BILL: Maybe.

PISTON: Or maybe they're both in it together!

BELLA: Like, they're each half a werewolf?

PISTON: No, I mean...

BILL: Or they maybe do it part time!

PISTON: No...

BELLA: Or like a time share!

PISTON: No, I mean they're both... *(Makes ambiguous gesture with his hands)* somehow...in it together somehow...

BELLA: You mean, like... *(Makes ambiguous gesture with her hands)*

PISTON: *(Frustrated:)* All right, I don't know what I mean! None of this makes any sense. I thought Biedermann was the werewolf. But he wasn't, and now I don't know what to think. But there's something fishy here, and I'm gonna find out what it is!

(BILL *tries to sneak the fish to* BELLA. *She gestures for him to put it back in his pocket.*)

PISTON: Helga Hermosa and Larry Fingers both
suddenly check out of the hotel right after they're
cleared of the murder. Alfredo Centauri vanishes
without a trace, and Wolfgang Biedermann ends up
an innocent victim of bullets that mysteriously change
from silver to lead. Nothing adds up. And when you
do add it up, you get zero, and that's still nothing.
So you're right back at square one. Which is the
loneliest number. Okay, I'm giving myself a headache.
...All right, first things first. There's a werewolf on the
loose in this hotel. Or maybe not. Maybe it checked out.
But either way, we've got to warn the other guests.
(He starts to leave.)

BELLA: But—

PISTON: *(Stopping in the doorway:)* And Cabal can
terminate me if she doesn't like it! I won't have another
murder on my conscience. *(He leaves.)*

BELLA: They checked out.

(PISTON comes back.)

PISTON: What?

BELLA: They checked out.

PISTON: Who?

BELLA: The other guests.

PISTON: Which other guests?

BELLA: All of 'em, I think.

BILL: Uh huh.

PISTON: *All* the other guests checked out?

BELLA & BILL: Uh huh.

PISTON: Why?

*(BELLA and BILL shrug. He glares at both of them,
several times.)*

PISTON: Are there any other mysterious goings-on I should know about?

BILL: Hotel's on fire.

PISTON: What?

(BELLA *glares at* BILL.)

BILL: Nothin'.

(PISTON *sizes them both up again, suspicious.*)

PISTON: Would you two excuse me for a moment?

(BILL *and* BELLA *leave.*)

PISTON: *(To the audience:)* When did I first suspect that Cabal the hotel manager was responsible for the latest disappearances? *(Suddenly realizing:)* My God, that's it! Cabal the hotel manager must be responsible! I've been barking up the proverbial wrong tree. But I'm onto her now. When every guest in the hotel suddenly disappears without an explanation, there's only one explanation. *(He draws his gun and bounds out of the room. He scrambles back in and slams the door behind him.)* The hotel's on fire!!

(*Freeze.* HARLEQUIN *enters. Looks at* PISTON.)

HARLEQUIN: Wouldn't want to be in your shoes.

ROME—TWELVE B C

(ALFREDO *meets with the other Roman Centurions.*)

ALFREDO: Send the first legion along the south slope, and bring up the archers.

THIRD CENTURION: What about the Tuscan mercenaries?

ALFREDO: Tell them to wait below. If it is his destiny to die today, it will be with a Roman shaft in his heart.

(*The* THIRD CENTURION *rushes off to carry out his orders.*)

(The SECOND CENTURION *is examining the gold crucifix apprehensively.)*

SECOND CENTURION: I fear it may be our destiny to die today.

ALFREDO: Marcus Benignus—

SECOND CENTURION: We don't know what this is!! We don't know what god we've defiled!!

*(*ALFREDO *puts his sword to the* SECOND CENTURION*'s throat.)*

ALFREDO: The only god that is going to be defiled today is the god of cowardly Roman soldiers who babble and whimper like children!

*(*SECOND CENTURION *falls silent.)*

ALFREDO: Do you know the name of this place?

SECOND CENTURION: Athanos.

ALFREDO: *(Significantly:)* "The place without death." So, you see, nobody is going to die today.

(Pause, and then they both laugh. ALFREDO *puts his sword away.)*

SECOND CENTURION: I wish you could always say that with such confidence.

ALFREDO: Come, we'll stand watch together.

(They stand watch.)

(Pause)

ALFREDO: Can I ask you something, Marcus Benignus?

SECOND CENTURION: Anything, Centurion.

ALFREDO: *(Seductively:)* Do you think it's immoral?

SECOND CENTURION: What?

ALFREDO: The eating of snails.

SECOND CENTURION: *(Warily:)* The eating of snails?

ALFREDO: Yes.

SECOND CENTURION: Do I think it's immoral?

ALFREDO: Yes.

(Nervous pause.)

SECOND CENTURION: Why? Do you have some snails?

ALFREDO: Only a handful.

SECOND CENTURION: Where are they?

ALFREDO: In my pocket.

(Nervous pause, SECOND CENTURION *looks to see that no one's coming.)*

SECOND CENTURION: Let me taste one.

*(*ALFREDO *digs in his pocket. The* SECOND CENTURION *looks on, fascinated.* HARLEQUIN *comes over and, leaning in to get a better view, places a hand on the* SECOND CENTURION'*s shoulder.)*

SECOND CENTURION: *(Suddenly alert:)* Did you hear something?

ALFREDO: No.

SECOND CENTURION: Wait a minute, where are we?

ALFREDO: Athanos. Outside of Rome.

SECOND CENTURION: No, it looks like Athanos outside of Rome, but...

ALFREDO: Is something wrong?

SECOND CENTURION: What year is it?

ALFREDO: What year?

SECOND CENTURION: *(With mounting hysteria:)* The year, man, what's the year!?!

ALFREDO: 12 B C. Why—?

SECOND CENTURION: B C?!? Do you know what that means?!?

ALFREDO: "Before Christ", isn't it?

SECOND CENTURION: *(Shrieking out of control:)* WHO THE HELL IS CHRIST?!??!?! Great Jupiter, we're a flashback! We're living in a flashback! None of this is really happening. We're just reliving the past so someone in the future can go on with their story. But what about us? What about me? Don't I have a story? Do I make general? Command a Roman legion? What about my family? My children? Do I have children? Where am I now? Am I famous? Or am I already dead? Rotting in some Tunisian desert or sunk in a galley at the bottom of the Nile? *(To the audience:)* What happens to me? Somebody please tell me! *(Beat)* They just sit there. They don't know! They don't know me. Maybe I'm not even a main character. Maybe I'm just the Second Centurion—part of the human backdrop against which the real characters play their hour upon life's stage. After this scene I don't even exist! Is that it? Oh, please, God, don't let me be a flashback. I WANT A LIFE, TOO! I have hopes, dreams, aspirations. I'm complex! I'm fascinating! Oh, God! Oh, God! I'm going into post-traumatic shock! *(He goes into post-traumatic shock.)*

(ALFREDO *is completely baffled.*)

HARLEQUIN: Last time I do that.

(Lights fade on the CENTURIONS.*)*

(HARLEQUIN *looks at* PISTON.*)*

PISTON: *(Suddenly unfreezing:)* HELP! HELP! The hotel's on fire!!

(The WEREWOLF *enters behind* PISTON, *and chloroforms him.)*

BLACKOUT

EPISODE 5

"Do you mind if I take off my clothes?"

CHARACTERS

HARLEQUIN
SPIKE
LARRY FINGERS
TODD MORTON
FANTASY CHICK
DICK PISTON
HERBERTO HERMOSA
WOLFGANG BIEDERMANN

HARLEQUIN

HARLEQUIN: LARRY AND THE WEREWOLF. Episode Five! Awooooo...

LARRY FINGERS AND SPIKE

(Lights up on SPIKE, *dressed as the Thai goddess of flaming death, but with an eyepatch and a crucifix.)*

SPIKE: *(Sings:)* If I never see tomorrow,
I have lived enough today
For a thousand thousand lifetimes
I can throw this one away.

If tomorrow I'm forgotten,
Please remember only this:
That today at least you loved me
That we parted with a kiss.

If I never see tomorrow,
This is all I want to say:

DAMMIT! You did it again! *(To* LARRY:*)* You're flat on "tomorrow" every time. And when you're flat, it looks like I'm off key. And I'm not off key, you are!! *(She paces, fuming.)* Jesus Christ...

(She paces. No response from LARRY, *who keeps playing some weird atonal amblings.)*

SPIKE: Well??? *(Still no response)* Larry? *(Softening:)* I'm sorry I yelled at you, Larry. It's just that this audition is so important to me. If we get this deal... *(Stops making excuses:)* I'm sorry, Larry. It's like you say, I should just

trust you, I know. And I do. I do trust you, Larry.
With my life, I trust you. More than that, with my...
With my other stuff, you know. And I just want you
to know that... That, that, that...I love...working with
you, and I hope you understand that if I'm moody
sometimes... Well, it's not because I'm going to kill you.
Oh God no, Larry, I would never do that! It's just that
I want this record deal so much. But I guess we all do.
I'm sorry. *(Pause)* I'm glad we had this talk. *(Pause)*
Shall we take it again?

(But LARRY *is still noodling atonally.)*

SPIKE: Is there something else that's bothering you,
Larry? Did something happen at that hotel that you're
not telling me about? Larry?

(She turns off his keyboard. He stops playing.)

SPIKE: Larry, you can talk to me.

*(*TODD *runs in.)*

TODD: The guy from the record company just pulled up!

SPIKE: Fuck off, Todd.

DICK PISTON'S DREAM

(The FANTASY CHICK *appears in a sweltering spot.)*

FANTASY CHICK: I think someone is after me.
A man.
I don't know why.
I don't know what he wants.
(She begins unbuttoning her blouse.)
But he's always there.
Lurking. Leering. Alluring.
Following
Like an afterthought.
So close

I can feel his
presence.
Like a smouldering shadow.
Like a dream. Only warmer.
Do you mind if I take off my clothes?
I'm so hot.
I feel like the room is on fire.
Is it just me? Or do you feel it too?

A ROOM IN A BURNING HOTEL

PISTON: *(Waking suddenly:)* Oh God, the hotel's on fire!
(He runs to the window.) HELP! HELP! The hotel's on
fire! *(Gets an idea:)* My cellular phone! *(Searches for his
cellular phone, but it's not there:)* My cellular phone!!
(Feeling his pockets:) My gun! My wallet! My underwear!
(Looks in his pants) No, I have my underwear. Okay,
gotta think. How long was I asleep? *(Looks at his watch:)*
My watch! *(It's gone, too.)* I can't believe I was mugged
in a burning hotel! And yet, that's what happened.
(Aside to the audience:) That's when I knew I was onto
something. Something big. Or something small with
really big repercussions. Maybe I was about to discover
the Werewolf's identity. Or maybe I'm just in over my
proverbial head. So many maybe's. But one thing's for
sure. I won't find the answers trapped in a burning
hotel. Gotta think. Gotta ask myself, what would Dick
Piston do in this situation? *(He looks out the window.)*
If this were a movie, I'd leap out this window. And just
before I hit the pavement, a truck full of goosedown
would pull into the alley below. But it's not a movie.
(He looks toward the door.) If this were one of my novels,
right about now, there'd be a knock at the door. But it's
not a novel.

(Knock at the door. PISTON is not sure what to make of this. Another knock at the door. PISTON apprehensively goes to the door and opens it. The ghosts burst in.)

HERMOSA: Wooo...!

BIEDERMANN: We brought chips!

PISTON: Oh, God, no!

HERMOSA: Wooo! Where's the card table?

BIEDERMANN: Out in the hall.

(HERMOSA goes out to get the card table.)

BIEDERMANN: I got pretzels, and soda...

PISTON: What are you two doing here?

BIEDERMANN & HERMOSA: WE'RE HAUNTING YOU!

HERMOSA: Boy, he's a little slow on the uptake.

BIEDERMANN: Yer tellin' me? *(To PISTON:)* How many times did you shoot me?

HERMOSA: Five or six times, wasn't it?

BIEDERMANN: Five or six times he shoots me. And I'm not even a werewolf!

PISTON: You look like a werewolf!

BIEDERMANN: Grrr!

(BIEDERMANN lunges at PISTON. HERMOSA jumps between them.)

HERMOSA: Hey, hey, hey!

(He separates them.)

HERMOSA: All right, who's gonna be the bigger man?

BIEDERMANN: I'm sorry Piston. I guess I overreacted when you called me a werewolf, because I was mad because you killed me in cold blood. But, it's okay, I'm over it now. I forgive you. And I'm sorry I growled at you.

HERMOSA: Great! Let's play cards!

PISTON: So are you going to stop haunting me now?

BIEDERMANN: Are you kidding? This is the most fun I've had all week.

HERMOSA: Hey, Piston, you got any money? We're ghosts.

PISTON: And I'm trapped in a burning building!

HERMOSA: Yeah, but give us your wallet.

PISTON: My wallet was stolen!

HERMOSA: Oh. *(To* BIEDERMANN:*)* Now what?

BIEDERMANN: We'll play strip poker. Piston, are you in?

PISTON: You stupid ghosts have picked a very inconvenient time to be haunting me.

BIEDERMANN: Nah, this is perfect. Wooo! *(Ghostly:)* You realize you wouldn't be in this mess if you hadn't let the murderer get away. *(Pokerly:)* I'll take two.

HERMOSA: Dealer takes three.

PISTON: I'm trying to catch the real murderer, but it ain't gonna happen if I don't get out of this hotel alive. Did you ever think of that?

BIEDERMANN: Pair o' tens.

HERMOSA: Pair o' kings. Gimme your shirt. Wooo!

(BIEDERMANN *takes off his shirt.*)

PISTON: You know, except for when I was unconscious just now, I haven't had a minute of sleep since you started haunting me. I'm not gonna bring anybody to justice with you two distracting me.

HERMOSA: You're not gonna bring anybody to justice if you don't get out of this hotel.

(*The ghosts laugh.*)

BIEDERMANN: Two.

HERMOSA: Three.

PISTON: Okay, my point exactly. If I don't find a way out of this hotel, I'm going to burn to death. Will that make you happy?

BIEDERMANN & HERMOSA: YES! Woooo!

BIEDERMANN: Serve you right if you did die. Two pair.

HERMOSA: Damn.

(HERMOSA *takes off his shirt.*)

BIEDERMANN: You know what it feels like being shot five or six times? It's five or six times worse than being shot once, which is no picnic.

HERMOSA: That's nothing. Have you ever had your throat torn out?

BIEDERMANN: Ouch.

HERMOSA: First imagine getting a really bad shave...

PISTON: I didn't tear your throat out!

HERMOSA: Oh. Well, somebody did. (*Ghostly:*) And what are you going to do about it?

PISTON: I'm going to ignore the two of you from now on.

BIEDERMANN: Ah, come on! Here, let me deal you a hand.

PISTON: No.

HERMOSA: Yeah, deal him in.

BIEDERMANN: Is it just me, or is it getting hot in here?

HERMOSA: Hmm. Check the thermostat.

BIEDERMANN: Oh, you know what? I bet it's because the hotel's on fire.

HERMOSA: I bet you're right. We better up the stakes.

BIEDERMANN: Piston, this hand's for two items of clothing.

PISTON: I can't hear you.

HERMOSA: I fold. Piston?

PISTON: Leave me alone.

HERMOSA: I'll play his hand. Whoo-ee! I'll see your two, and raise you two items of clothing.

BIEDERMANN: Wow. Four items of clothing. All right, I'm in. How many cards, Piston?

HERMOSA: One.

BIEDERMANN: Dealer takes three. Okay, what does he got?

HERMOSA: Queen high. How 'bout you?

BIEDERMANN: Full house.

HERMOSA: You just lost four items of clothing, Piston. Pay up.

PISTON: No.

BIEDERMANN: Aw, c'mon, take off your clothes.

PISTON: Make me.

HERMOSA: Shall I?

BIEDERMANN: Please.

(HERMOSA *mimes unbuttoning his shirt, causing* PISTON *to unbutton his own shirt.*)

PISTON: What's going on?

BIEDERMANN: Corporeal possession. Sit back and enjoy the ride.

PISTON: Stop it! Stop it!

(PISTON, *still undressing, runs over and kicks* HERMOSA.)

HERMOSA: Ow.

PISTON: You stupid ghosts!

BIEDERMANN: *(Laughing hysterically:)* Hey, Piston,
what's your mom gonna think when they find you
in the hotel burned to a crisp and stark naked?

(PISTON *chases* HERMOSA *around the room, while they both
continue to undress. After awhile,* PISTON *gives up, and just
stands there being undressed while* BIEDERMANN *and*
HERMOSA *chuckle wildly.)*

PISTON: I hate the two of you so much right now.
I feel bad about the things that have happened to you,
but this is ridiculous. Hermosa, if you weren't dead
already, I'd kill you myself. And Biedermann, I'd kill
you myself but I killed you myself already.

BIEDERMANN: *(Laughing hysterically:)* Don't worry,
you're killin' me now!

PISTON: All right, we'll see who gets the last laugh.

(PISTON, *his pants down around his ankles, charges across
the room and hurls himself out the window.* BIEDERMANN
stops laughing.)

BIEDERMANN: Oh shit.

(BIEDERMANN *and* HERMOSA *go over to the window and
look out.)*

BIEDERMANN & HERMOSA: Ew.

BIEDERMANN: Who we gonna haunt now?

BLACKOUT

EPISODE 6

"I told you not to call me here..."

CHARACTERS

HARLEQUIN
CABAL
LARRY FINGERS
TODD MORTON
SPIKE
SECOND CENTURION
ALFREDO CENTAURI
HELGA HERMOSA

HARLEQUIN

(HARLEQUIN *enters with a telephone and places it on a table at centerstage.*)

HARLEQUIN: LARRY AND THE WEREWOLF. Episode Six! Awooooo...

(*The telephone rings.*)

CABAL'S APARTMENT

(CABAL *rushes in from the shower and snatches up the phone.*)

CABAL: Did you kill him?! Is he dead?! ...Oh, hello officer. ...A fire? At my hotel? Really? And you suspect arson? ...Oh, you don't? Forget I mentioned it. ...Uh huh. ...Uh huh. (*Bored:*) Yeah yeah yeah, devastated by the news. Listen, there wasn't anyone trapped in the fire, was there? About five foot, ten inches", hundred eighty pounds? ...No reason, just curious. It would just be such a shame if someone like that was trapped inside. Prime of his life and all. And with the new book coming out this fall. No, wait, he never finished the book. Forget I mentioned it. (*She quickly hangs up the phone and exits.*)

LARRY'S STUDIO

(The phone rings. LARRY enters and stares at the phone, as it continues to ring. Finally, he decides to answer it. But just as he picks up the receiver, TODD walks in, so LARRY hangs up.)

TODD: Three minutes, Larry.

(TODD walks out. LARRY picks up the receiver again, but the caller is gone, and he puts it back down. SPIKE enters.)

SPIKE: Who was that on the phone? Larry? It was that caller again, wasn't it? Oh my God! How did he get this number?! It's unlisted! ...Or she. I mean, we just rented the studio this morning! It's like he knows our every move. ...Or she. All right, we can't let this upset us. We've got an audition in three minutes.

(SPIKE can tell that LARRY is disturbed by the phone call.)

SPIKE: Larry? You let it upset you, didn't you? I told ya, when he calls, you gotta just hang up and call the police. ...Or she.

(The phone rings. SPIKE grabs it right away and screams into the receiver...)

SPIKE: LEAVE US ALONE, YOU PSYCHO! YOU SICK, TWISTED GHOUL!! *(She slams the phone down.)* See? And now I'm calling the police. Hello? 9-1-1? I want to report a prank phone call. *(Suddenly she puts down the phone, realizing:)* Larry! I know who's doing this! It's Todd! He's the one!

(She thinks for a moment and realizes TODD is in the studio with them and couldn't possibly be making the calls.)

SPIKE: Well, maybe not, but I say we get rid of him anyway. Just to be safe. *(Beat)* ...Oh. ...I don't mean that the way it sounds. I don't mean we should beat him to death with a pipe, sever his head, hands and feet, and throw them in a ravine. Those days are behind me, Larry. *(She sobs.)* Can we not talk about this now? Can't you see it upsets me? And we have an audition in three minutes. *(She turns away, sobbing quietly.)*

(Without a word, LARRY *walks out of the studio.* TODD *comes in.)*

TODD: Two minutes, Spike. *(He goes out.)*

CABAL'S APARTMENT

*(*CABAL *is anxiously waiting for a phone call. The phone rings.* CABAL *snatches it up.)*

CABAL: Did you kill him?! Is he dead?! *(Beat)* WHY DO YOU KEEP CALLING HERE??? ...What do you mean, I sound suspicious?! Of course I sound suspicious! You'd be suspicious, too, if someone burned your hotel down! No, wait, it was an accident, wasn't it? Well, that's even worse! Y'know, you think you know a building, and then it does something like this. And then there's the two dead guys! There are only two that you know of, right, officer? Good, good. Well, see? Two dead? Burning building? It doesn't take a rocket psychiatrist to tell me someone's out to get me. I'm the victim here! But now on top of everything I've got the cops calling to harrass me when you oughta be out saving lives or fighting crime or whatever it is you do with all those doughnuts!! *(Silence)* ...Apology accepted. *(She hangs up.)*

THE SECOND CENTURION

(The SECOND CENTURION *armed with a spear, standing sentry. He looks out across the horizon. The phone rings.* SECOND CENTURION *tries to ignore it. It rings again. The* SECOND CENTURION *picks up the phone.)*

SECOND CENTURION: I told you not to call me here.
I can't talk now. ...You are? ...I can't. ...You are? Well...
(He checks to see that no one is coming.) What are you
wearing? ...Mm hmm. ...Mmm... *(He doublechecks to see
that no one is coming.)* I am touching you... I am pulling
you close to me... I am kissing you on the— ...WHAT!?
Well, then I am slapping *you!* ...Well, I am killing you,
too!! I am stabbing you to death with my big wooden
spear!! You bitch! Don't ever call me again—!

(Just then, ALFREDO *enters. He is in modern dress.)*

SECOND CENTURION: *(Continuing, calmly:)* ...because we
are satisfied with our long distance service.

(He hangs up the phone and turns to ALFREDO. *Pause.*
ALFREDO *smiles.)*

ALFREDO: I have not seen this outfit in a very long time.

(Pause)

SECOND CENTURION: Does it make you hungry?

ALFREDO: Snails?

SECOND CENTURION: A few.

(Lights fade.)

A STREET CORNER

*(*HARLEQUIN *transforms the telephone into a pay phone.*
HELGA *rushes on, frazzled, clutching her box of jewelry.)*

HELGA: I've got to find him. I've got to find him! But
who? Who?! I'm so lousy with names. *(Then suddenly...)*
What's that? *(She senses something.)* I feel like I'm being
followed... I feel like I'm being watched... I feel like I'm
being undressed with someone's eyes.

*(*HARLEQUIN *quickly averts eyes.)*

HELGA: Now it's gone. *(She giggles.)* Just my
imagination. Oh, and there's a bunny!

*(HELGA follows the bunny offstage. She comes back, points at
the pay phone.)*

HELGA: Wait! A pay phone! If I can get to that pay
phone, I can call him! *(With a heroic effort, she gets to
the pay phone.)* YES! *(And then:)* No! I don't know his
number. Wait, he gave me his number! *(She searches
in her pockets, and finds a scrap of paper, unfolds it....)* No,
he gave me a kleenex. *(She gets an idea:)* The operator!
(She calls the operator.) Hello, operator, can you help me?
This is an emergency! I need his number right away!
(Pause) You know..."him". Him! Well, if I knew that I
wouldn't need your help! You're just mad because you
don't know! You don't, do you? Just admit it, you don't
know his number either! *(She hangs up.)* Well, he's just
going to have to call *me*. *(She waits for the phone to ring.)*
Oooooh! Why doesn't he call??? *(She looks at her watch.)*
And now I'm late for work. *(She goes off. She comes back.)*
But what if I go and he comes and I'm gone? I have
to leave him a note. I have to leave him a note! That's
fun to say. *(She writes him a note.)* "Dear..." *(She can't
remember his name.)* "...sir." *(She thinks.)* "I waited and
waited and waited, but you never came. Not even once.
...So I am leaving you. ...If you receive this note, please
do not try to follow me." *(She chews on the end of her
pencil.)* "...Or the trail of gemstones which I am leaving
for you." *(She leaves the note by the phone and goes off,
dropping a trail of jewelry behind her.)*

*(A few moments later, LARRY comes in from the other side
and finds the note on the phone. He crumples it into a ball
and goes back out the way he came.)*

CABAL'S APARTMENT

(CABAL *is anxiously waiting for a phone call. The phone rings.* CABAL *decides to answer the phone discreetly this time*)

CABAL: Hello? ...Bella? (*And then:*) Did you kill him?! Is he dead?! He jumped out a window??? Bella, you idiot, that's two jumpers in one day, no one's gonna believe that. Oh, he really did jump out a window? Could you make it look like he was pushed? We don't want people to get suspicious. He didn't happen to rip his guts out on the way down? Because that would be perfect. ...I guess that was too much to hope for. Well, at least he's dead. He's *not* dead? You're telling Piston fell ten stories and got up and walked away? They scraped him up and took him away? Well, at least that's something. He's in a coma? That's perfect, he's helpless! I want you and Bill to go down to the hospital and finish the job. Oh, and Bella, try to make it look like a suicide.

BLACKOUT

EPISODE 7

"Our work here is done. Let's go do some nurses."

CHARACTERS

HARLEQUIN
SPIKE
TODD MORTON
SHADOWY FIGURE
WOLFGANG BIEDERMANN
HERBERTO HERMOSA
HELGA HERMOSA
BILL BOLA
BELLA BOLA

HARLEQUIN

HARLEQUIN: LARRY AND THE WEREWOLF. Episode Seven! Awooooo...

LARRY'S STUDIO

(SPIKE *is pacing anxiously, occasionally glancing out the door.* TODD *enters.)*

TODD: One minute, Spike.

SPIKE: He's gone.

TODD: What?

SPIKE: Gone.

TODD: Who?

SPIKE: Larry!

TODD: Fingers?

SPIKE: He's gone.

TODD: Larry's gone?

SPIKE: Larry's gone!

TODD: Larry *Fingers*?

SPIKE: Larry Fingers! Larry's gone!

TODD: He left, he's gone?

SPIKE: He left!

TODD: Larry *left*?

SPIKE: Larry left!

TODD: Left the building?

SPIKE: Yes! The building! He left the building! Larry left the building! He's gone! Larry's gone! Larry's gone!

(SPIKE *is hysterical.* TODD *slaps her. She falls silent.*)

TODD: We've got to stay calm. Try not to panic. We've got less than a minute to—urk!

(SPIKE *is strangling* TODD.)

TODD: *(Gasps:)* Spi—!

(*She still strangles him.*)

TODD: Spi—!

(*She lets him go.* TODD *gasps.*)

TODD: The guy from the record company is already here!

(SPIKE *rummages in a box of music equipment.*)

TODD: We've got to figure out what we're gonna do when he— Urk!

(SPIKE *is strangling* TODD *with some electronic cable.*)

SPIKE: Don't...ever...touch me!

(*The door to the studio slams open. A shadowy figure stands silhouetted in the doorway.* SPIKE *and* TODD *both turn to look at him. The shadowy figure looks at his watch. He looks at* SPIKE *and* TODD. SPIKE *lets* TODD *go.*)

SPIKE: I'll get in costume.

PISTON'S HOSPITAL ROOM

(PISTON, *covered in bandages, lies in a coma as* BIEDERMANN *and* HERMOSA *look on.*)

BIEDERMANN: This takes all the fun out of it.

HERMOSA: Yup. (*He is snacking on some hospital food.*)

BIEDERMANN: Well, let's go haunt some nurses.
(*He starts toward the door.*)

HERMOSA: Waitaminute! You can't just walk out now.

BIEDERMANN: You wanna go through the wall?

HERMOSA: What about Piston?

BIEDERMANN: You don't expect me to carry him?

HERMOSA: Piston was our only hope!

BIEDERMANN: Hope for what?

HERMOSA: For finding our killers.

BIEDERMANN: *Your* killer. The only hope of finding *your* killer. *Piston* killed me.

HERMOSA: Oh... Right.

BIEDERMANN: I mean, if I want to watch a body rot, I can go back to the morgue and watch mine. At least *that* would be theatrical. (*Beat*) Hey, you wanna do that? I bet we're all green now.

HERMOSA: Oh, great, talk about my guts while I'm eating!

(*Just then,* BIEDERMANN *sees someone offstage.*)

BIEDERMANN: Hermosa, come here quick!

(HERMOSA *runs to the door.*)

BIEDERMANN: Do you see what I see?

HERMOSA: What?

BIEDERMANN: That nurse.

HERMOSA: You think she looks suspicious?

BIEDERMANN: I think she looks *hot.*

HERMOSA: (*Disgusted with him:*) Oh, please!

BIEDERMANN: What? You don't think she's hot?

HERMOSA: Biedermann, you say that about *everyone.*
Your mind's in the gutter.

BIEDERMANN: My mind is not in the gutter! It's in that
woman's blouse. ...And now it's unfastening her bra.

(Offstage sound of a surprised nurse)

HERMOSA: What hormones are you on?

BIEDERMANN: It's called desperation, Herbie.

HERMOSA: You've only been gone one day.

BIEDERMANN: Easy for you to say. You died in action.
Look at me. You know how often I got laid? Halloween!
Now I don't even have *that* to look forward to. *(To
offstage nurses:)* Awoo!! Baby! Poppa wants a sponge
bath!

*(*BIEDERMANN *grabs the call button and rings for a nurse.)*

HERMOSA: How do you know I died in action?

BIEDERMANN: Hey, I looked out the window. I saw the
body. *Somebody* took a bite outta crime.

*(*HERMOSA *cringes.)*

BIEDERMANN: And I mean... *(Chomping and shaking his
head like a dog with a chew toy:)* GNARRR!!

HERMOSA: *(Remembering:)* Ow, ow, ow.

BIEDERMANN: And unless that was self-inflicted—

HERMOSA: No comment.

BIEDERMANN: —I'd say someone out there is always
gonna remember you as quite a mouthful. Whereas I,
on the other hand, died fully clothed in a roomful of
total strangers. *(Afterthought:)* Although that Helga
chick was hot. So what do you say? Our work here is

done. Let's go do some nurses. *(Looking out the door:)* Here comes one! Hide!

(HERMOSA and BIEDERMANN hide behind the bed and peer at the approaching nurse.)

BIEDERMANN: *(Waxing poetic:)* She walked into my world like a dream. Only wetter. *(Poking PISTON* Hey, Piston, are you writing this down?

HERMOSA: Hey, that nurse *is* kinda hot.

BIEDERMANN: She was a vision in white. Angelic. Medicinal. Waitaminute. That's no nurse.

(HELGA enters, dressed as a nurse.)

BIEDERMANN: That's your wife.

HERMOSA: I thought she looked familiar.

LARRY'S STUDIO

(A shadowy Figure sits in a folding chair. TODD enters, shakes his hand.)

TODD: I just want to thank you—and I know you asked me not to touch you, but—to thank you again for coming. And for waiting. For coming and waiting, it'll be just another minute, and I'm sorry I touched you, just another minute and we'll be ready and so I just, on behalf of all of us—Larry and Spike and myself— did I introduce myself? Todd Morton, we spoke on the phone—on behalf of all of us, how much we appreciate this opportunity—and especially Larry—how much we—and Spike—how much—and me—how much we all appreciate you giving us this chance to show you what it is that we do. And do so well, I might add, but you'll see that for yourself I think, and I think the music speaks for itself so without any further ado... Can I get you something to drink while you're waiting? Tea, iced tea, water, soda, soda water, anything? Coffee, blowjob, anything? Just kidding, little joke. Blowjob, that's a joke. Unless that's what you want. Did you want a blowjob, because— well, never mind, it was a joke, I'll just— anything, you name it, okay? You name it, and you got it, and I'll be right back.

PISTON'S HOSPITAL ROOM

(BIEDERMANN, HERMOSA, HELGA *and a comatose* PISTON, *as before.*)

HELGA: Did you buzz me, Misterrrrr...? *(She goes to the foot of the bed and reads his chart:)* Piston? *(Lost in thought for a moment:)* ...Dick. ...Piston.

BIEDERMANN: *(Aside to* HERMOSA:*)* What is it?

(HERMOSA *shrugs.*)

HELGA: That name... It's like...a powerful piece of greasy machinery. And part of a car. Oh my God, Dick Piston! *(She dives onto the bed and begins clawing the bandages from* PISTON's *face.)* Mister Piston! Mister Piston! *(She claws the bandages free, revealing* PISTON's *feet. She screams!)*

BIEDERMANN: That's a nasty case of athlete's head.

HERMOSA: I can't believe I married this woman.

(HELGA *turns around and claws at the other end of* PISTON. *Meanwhile* PISTON *begins spasming violently.*)

HELGA: Mister Piston! It's me Helga! Helga Hermosa!

(PISTON *lurches and gags.* HELGA *listens.*)

HELGA: What? What? What are you trying to tell me?

(BIEDERMANN *and* HERMOSA *gesture hintingly at the heart monitor which is bleeping wildly as* PISTON *convulses.*)

HELGA: I don't understand what you're saying.
"Wauuh"? "Oowaugh"? Oh, I don't know, Mister
Piston. ...Sounds a dog makes? ...Things you say when
you're choking? *(Finally, she notices the heart monitor.)*
Oh! Oh my! Doctor! Doctor! I need a doctor stat!
(Still straddling PISTON, *she tries to perform C P R.)*
Stat! Extreeeeemely stat! Hold on, Mister Piston,
help is on the way.

(Enter BELLA *and* BILL, *disguised as surgeons.)*

HELGA: Doctor! Mister Piston has gone into convulsions.

BELLA: Nurse... Get off the patient.

*(*HELGA *climbs off of* PISTON. *His spasms stop.)*

HELGA: Oh, that's better.

BILL: *(Pointing at* PISTON:*)* Can I ride the—

*(*BELLA *elbows him.)*

BELLA: Nurse, we'll take it from here.

HELGA: Don't worry, Mister Piston, you're in good
hands now. *(She starts to leave, but comes back.)* Um,
Mister Piston, I know this isn't the best time, but I really
need to speak to you. Could you please call me as soon
as you... *(Looks at* PISTON's *chart.)* ...come out of your
coma. *(She writes down her phone number and slips it
between* PISTON's *bandages.)* If a man answers, don't
say anything, just hang up. *(She exits.)*

BIEDERMANN: *(To* HERMOSA:*)* I say we haunt *her*!

LARRY'S STUDIO

TODD: *(Voice over:)* Ladieeeeeeees and Gentlemen!
Larrrrrry Fingers! aaaaaaaaaand Spike!

(Beat. Enter TODD.*)*

TODD: Okay, now what normally would happen here, is...

SHADOWY FIGURE: Where's Larry Fingers?

TODD: Okay, see, we're having a little prob—

SHADOWY FIGURE: I came to see Fingers.

(SPIKE *enters from the stage area.*)

SPIKE: um, Mister, uh, sir, uh, Larry...he...

TODD: He's gonna be right back...

SPIKE: He's not...uh...

TODD: But we're gonna start with a few of Spike's numbers—

SPIKE: I can do my a cappella numbers.

TODD: Just to warm you up, and then—

SHADOWY FIGURE: I want Fingers! Fingers! Fingers is the talent! Fingers is the show!

SPIKE: But, sir. I can—

SHADOWY FIGURE: Fingers! Show me Fingers! You are nothing! Without Fingers, you are nothing!

(SPIKE *is stunned.* TODD's *a little stunned, too.* SHADOWY FIGURE *storms out, slamming the door behind him.*)

TODD: *(Under his breath:)* I'll show you some fingers, you wacko...

(SPIKE *faints.*)

PISTON'S HOSPITAL ROOM

(BIEDERMANN *is at the door, ready to leave.* HERMOSA *is morbidly fascinated with* BELLA *and* BILL *who stand over the comatose* PISTON.)

BILL: He looks so peaceful.

BIEDERMANN: Hermosa!

BILL: Sleeping like a baby.

BIEDERMANN: Hermosa!

BELLA: I always love babies.

BIEDERMANN: She's gettin' away!

BELLA: Nooooo defenses.

BIEDERMANN: Hermosa!

BELLA: Well, you wanna do it?

BILL: Me??

BELLA: *(Teasing:)* On second thought...

BILL: Oh, please please please, Bella, pleeeeeease.

(BELLA *reaches into her pocket and takes out a switchblade. She flicks it open and hands it to* BILL.)

BELLA: Careful, don't cut yourself.

(BILL *carefully takes the knife and is just about to plunge it into* PISTON'S *chest when Bella interrupts him.*)

BELLA: Ah, ah, ah! What did I tell you?

(BILL *stops, thinks, considers his options. Then with a pleased grin he uses the knife to cut* PISTON'S *blood supply.*)

BELLA: Gooood.

(As PISTON *begins to spasm,* BELLA *and* BILL *exit.* BILL
comes back in and places the knife in PISTON's *hand to make
it look like suicide. He exits.* PISTON *dies. Heart monitor goes
flatline....)*

BLACKOUT

EPISODE 8

"Is that a shotgun in your pocket, or am I one helluva dress?"

CHARACTERS

HARLEQUIN
DICK PISTON
HELGA HERMOSA
ALFREDO CENTAURI
LARRY FINGERS
FANTASY CHICK
SPIKE
TODD MORTON

PISTON'S HOSPITAL ROOM

(PISTON *lies dead in his hospital bed.* HARLEQUIN *enters and speaks to him.*)

HARLEQUIN: What must it be like for you to die?
Riddled with bullets.
Stabbed through the heart.
Tied up and tortured and torn limb from limb.

Caught in the explosion. Trapped in the wreckage.
Thrown from the jet...
And sucked into its engine.
It's all so picturesque.

None of this dull ache.
And sweating.
Itch.
Wearily surviving just one more...two more...
three more...decades.
Without a glorious blaze to go out in.
Romeo...Juliet...Elvis...
Even your deaths outstrip our lives.

LARRY AND THE WEREWOLF.

(HARLEQUIN *touches* PISTON. PISTON *sits up.*)

HARLEQUIN: Episode Eight!

PISTON'S DEATH VISIONS

(PISTON *looks at himself. He's dead.*)

PISTON: So I guess I never find out who really killed Herberto Hermosa. Curiosity—One. Proverbial cat—Zero. (*He gets out of bed.*) How did I know that I was dead? Was it the sudden sensation of serenity settling over me like a downy soft blanket of snow? Or the unexpected end to the constant, excruciating pain I'd been in from the moment I lept out of that hotel window? Well, maybe not from the window moment. But certainly from the moment ten stories later when I hit the ground, shattering every bone in my proverbial body. (*On second thought:*) No, actually, it *was* my body. ...Dammit that hurt. At least I got out of that burning hotel. ...Was it the feeling of floating, and a guy who looks a lot like me lying in the hospital bed below? Or the fact that I was up and around after only a day in traction? Or was it the bright white tunnel of light that seemed to beckon me into the hereafter?

(*A painfully bright light glares in* PISTON's *face.*)

PISTON: (*Flinching:*) Jesus Christ! Okay, it was the light.

HEAVENLY VOICES: (*Off:*) Pissstonnn...

PISTON: Be right there! (*To audience:*) You hear stories about people returning from the brink of death. Turning away from the tunnel of light and heading back to the land of the living. (*To the living:*) You stupid living! (*To the audience:*) Sorry, I'm a little pissed at them right now. It takes a strong will to go back. A strong will, and some unfinished business. (*Pause. He gazes longingly toward the land of the living:*) The detective in me says I can't leave the case unsolved. But I tell that detective: "You mean *you* can't leave the case unsolved!

Isn't that right, detective?! But what do I get out of it?
Me. Dick Piston." *(He sighs:)* ...hotel detective. I don't
like to walk away from a great mystery. But then...
(He turns in awe toward the tunnel of light.) What do you
call that?

*(*HELGA *appears.)*

HELGA: Piston...

PISTON: Helga?

HELGA: I'm your mother, Dick.

PISTON: Helga, you're not old enough to be my mother.

HELGA: I'm not Helga, Dick.

PISTON: But you look exactly like Helga Hermosa.
We must be related.

HELGA: Of course we're related, I'm your mother,
pay attention!

(She slaps him upside the head.)

PISTON: Not you, Ma, Helga! Am I related to Helga
Hermosa?

HELGA: *(Looking at her body:)* Oh, is that who this is?
Jesus Christ she dresses crappy. And she's gonna have
to do something about this hair. *(Looking in her pockets:)*
Silver bullets?

PISTON: Let me see those!

HELGA: No, they're mine. Back off! My body, my stuff.
*(Then she clears her throat and adopts the tone of a heavenly
vision:)* I have assumed the form of this prostitute—

PISTON: I think she's a nurse.

HELGA: Don't sass your mother. —Because, as you
recall, I abandoned you at birth and was killed shortly
thereafter in a bizarre trolley accident. So we've never
met.

PISTON: Uh huh.

HELGA: So if I came here looking like myself you wouldn't recognize me.

PISTON: Good point.

HELGA: Besides, they never found the head, so I'd be here going... "Mmck! *Mime mrr* mummer!" ...You think anyone's gonna follow *that* into the light?

PISTON: Not on an empty stomach.

HELGA: Y'see? *(Heavenly again:)* Come with me, Dick. Come into the light. Your grandparents are here. Your whole family. They'd love to meet you. Grammy Piston has an amazing scrap book. Did you know that your great great grandfather was the first man to impregnate—

(Her beeper goes off.)

HELGA: Whoops, that's all for now. Gotta go. See you on the other side. *(As she exits toward the light:)* Just follow the light. You'll get to an intersection that says, "RIGHT HERE FOR HELL". Don't go right. Keep left! *(She's gone.)*

PISTON: It was at that moment—

*(*ALFREDO *appears.)*

ALFREDO: Piston...

PISTON: Alfredo!

ALFREDO: No, I'm your dad.

PISTON: Dad?

ALFREDO: I abandoned you at birth and—

PISTON: Yeah, I got that from mom. Are you here to summon me into the light, too?

ALFREDO: Uh...yeah...uh...actually, I wanted to talk to you about your mother. Listen, whatever she tells you about me... It's not true, okay?

PISTON: uh...

ALFREDO: And I never pushed her in front of that trolley!!

PISTON: uh...

ALFREDO: I mean, Jesus Christ, there was a crowd, it was Mardi Gras, everybody was kinda... *(He jostles like a crowd.)* Is that my fault???

PISTON: Uh...

ALFREDO: Listen, you wanna hear my side of it, Grammy Piston knows where to find me, I gotta go.

(His beeper goes off.)

ALFREDO: See? *(Exiting:)* Don't go right at the intersection. That's hell. Keep left!

PISTON: *(Calling after him:)* Dad, your pockets! What's in your pockets?

(But ALFREDO is gone.)

HEAVENLY VOICES: Pissstonnn...

PISTON: My mother, my father, a family I'd never known. The answers to a lifetime of questions lay ahead of me. And if that weren't enough—

(LARRY appears crawling on hands and knees. LARRY rubs against PISTON's legs.)

PISTON: Fluffy?

(LARRY's beeper goes off, and he scampers off toward the light.)

PISTON: *(A little disturbed by that:)* Uh... And if that weren't enough... Behind me, I was leaving a lifetime of failure, frustration and unfinished novels. Plus a skeletal system that's gonna tell me the barometric pressure for the next *five* lifetimes. The hereafter calls me like the proverbial moth to the flame. The heretofore calls me like the proverbial telemarketer on a Friday night when you're in the shower getting ready for a big date, so you're dripping water all over the apartment, shampoo in your eyes, and all they want is for you to switch phone companies again, GOD I hate that!

HEAVENLY VOICES: Pissstonnn...

PISTON: *(Irritably, to the voices:)* Can I have one minute, please? It's not like I get a chance to do this again. *(To the audience:)* It was at that moment that the clincher walked into my life in high heels and fishnet stalkings, and a dress that screamed, "Is that a shotgun in your pocket, or am I one helluva dress?"

(The FANTASY CHICK appears in high heels and fishnet stalkings and one helluva dress.)

FANTASY CHICK: Dick Piston... I need you.

PISTON: And I need you to tell me you're not Grammy Piston.

(FANTASY CHICK kisses him, passionately.)

PISTON: Close enough.

FANTASY CHICK: Do you have a gun?

PISTON: No, that's just one helluva dress.

(FANTASY CHICK takes out a gun, checks the chamber and hands it to PISTON.)

FANTASY CHICK: Take mine. You'll need it.

PISTON: Do you have a beeper?

(FANTASY CHICK pulls a beeper out of her cleavage. PISTON grabs the beeper and smashes it to pieces. He takes the FANTASY CHICK in his arms and kisses her again.)

FANTASY CHICK: Come quickly.

PISTON: Beg your pardon?

FANTASY CHICK: We don't have much time. Follow me.

PISTON: Jesus Christ, if *you're* here, why does *anybody* go back?

(*She looks at him, faintly bewildered.*)

FANTASY CHICK: I'm not here.

(FANTASY CHICK *exits* away *from the light.* PISTON *is stunned.*)

LARRY'S STUDIO

(*When* LARRY *walks in,* SPIKE *and* TODD *are waiting for him.*)

TODD: Larry, where have you been?! The guy from the record company was here. You missed the audition!

SPIKE: (*Pushing* TODD *aside:*) Let me talk to him. (*To* LARRY:) What do you have to say for yourself, Larry?

TODD: Larry, he was furious! He's not coming back. You've blown the deal.

SPIKE: Back off, Todd!

(TODD *backs off.*)

SPIKE: I'd like a word with Larry, alone.

TODD: (*Edging out of the room:*) This is bad, Larry. Really bad.

(TODD *exits. Spike turns to* LARRY.)

SPIKE: I hope you're happy. (*Before he can react:*) Nuh! Don't even try that because I'm not gonna fall for it this time.

(LARRY *looks at her.*)

SPIKE: And don't give me those eyes, Larry, 'cause it won't work. I got the patch on the other side, and you know I can't see outta this one. We rehearsed this for weeks, Larry. I worked my ass off for this. All my life this is what I wanted. This was it. This was our big chance. I would kill for this. I'd die for this. I'd die and then come back and kill for this. That's how much I wanted this. That much. Let me finish. I wanted this for myself, I admit it, but I wanted it for you, too, Larry. For you and for me. For you and me, Larry, for us. That's who I wanted this for, Larry, for us. For both of us. For all of us. (*Beat. She realizes she doesn't want it for* TODD.) Well, for both of us. Larry...you and me...we really got something here. Something...you know... something...really...unspeakable. No, that's not the word. Well, you know what I'm trying to say, Larry. You know 'cause you said it yourself, a million times. ...But I guess that was just talk, huh, Larry? What is it with you, Larry? Is it drugs? Gambling? Is it—? Is it—? (*She sobs.*) ...Another woman? (*She begins sobbing uncontrollably.*) I know I got no dibs on you. I know you don't care nothin' about me. But Larry, please, I gotta know. Is that it? If you're gonna rip my heart out, you gotta do it now, Larry, 'cause I can't take any more lies!

(LARRY *puts a hand on her chest.* SPIKE *stops sobbing for a moment and switches the patch over to the other side.*)

SPIKE: Larry?

(LARRY *reaches into his pocket and pulls out a jewelry box and opens it. He shows it to* SPIKE. *It's an engagement ring.* SPIKE *looks at the ring, then at* LARRY, *then at the ring.* SPIKE *screams.* SPIKE *faints.*)

BLACKOUT

EPISODE 9

"Who told him about the furry serpent?"

CHARACTERS

HARLEQUIN
ALFREDO CENTAURI
MARCUS BENIGNUS
GAIUS LUCIUS
CABAL
BILL BOLA
BELLA BOLA
FANTASY DICK
FANTASY CHICK
DICK PISTON

HARLEQUIN

HARLEQUIN: LARRY AND THE WEREWOLF. Episode Nine! Awooooo...

MOUNTAINSIDE NEAR ROME

(A distant howl. ALFREDO *pricks up his ears. The* SECOND CENTURION—*Marcus Benignus*—*admires a gold ring given to him by* ALFREDO.*)*

MARCUS BENIGNUS: Centurion, I think it is not immoral.

ALFREDO: What?

MARCUS BENIGNUS: The eating of snails.

ALFREDO: You think it is not immoral?

MARCUS BENIGNUS: Why should one who eats snails be less moral than one who eats oysters? Or veal? I say we must be proud for what we are. Romans, centurions, and eaters of snail. Our silence is our death. Let us shout it from the mountaintops and echo it in the valley below. Let us proclaim it from the floor of the imperial senate and—!

ALFREDO: Silence, you fool!

*(*MARCUS BENIGNUS *falls silent. Pause)*

ALFREDO: Do you want someone to hear you?

*(*MARCUS BENIGNUS *shakes his head.)*

ALFREDO: I think you must be flogged for this outrage. *(He takes out a flog.)* Remove your tunic.

(MARCUS BENIGNUS *starts to take off his tunic.*)

ALFREDO: ...Slowly.

(MARCUS BENIGNUS *removes his tunic slowly, seductively. The* THIRD CENTURION—GAIUS LUCIUS—*enters.*)

GAIUS LUCIUS: Centurion?

ALFREDO: Gaius Lucius!

(MARCUS BENIGNUS *tries to cover himself.*)

GAIUS LUCIUS: Are you punishing Marcus Benignus?

ALFREDO: No. It was a misunderstanding.

MARCUS BENIGNUS: Yes. A misunderstanding.

ALFREDO: Some time ago Marcus Benignus was drunk in a Sicilian brothel, and he thought he'd gotten a tattoo.

MARCUS BENIGNUS: I see now I was mistaken.

(GAIUS LUCIUS *eyes them suspiciously.*)

GAIUS LUCIUS: I think you're punishing Marcus Benignus.

ALFREDO: It is not as it looks.

GAIUS LUCIUS: I think you are punishing Marcus Benignus unjustly! I think—

ALFREDO: Silence!

(GAIUS LUCIUS *falls silent.*)

ALFREDO: What you are suggesting is an outrage!

(GAIUS LUCIUS *starts to take off his tunic.*)

ALFREDO: Not now.

(GAIUS LUCIUS *stops taking off his tunic.*)

ALFREDO: We will not speak of this again.

GAIUS LUCIUS: Yes, Centurion.

ALFREDO: What news from the first legion?

GAIUS LUCIUS: We found him. But he escaped us.

MARCUS BENIGNUS: He escaped an entire Roman legion? How?!

GAIUS LUCIUS: He frightened us.

MARCUS BENIGNUS: He frightened an entire Roman legion?! How?!?

(GAIUS LUCIUS turns to ALFREDO...)

GAIUS LUCIUS: Why is he wearing your ring?

ALFREDO: It is not as it looks.

GAIUS LUCIUS: It looks like he's wearing your ring! It looks like you gave him your ring—!

ALFREDO: Silence!!

(GAIUS LUCIUS falls silent. ALFREDO takes GAIUS LUCIUS aside.)

ALFREDO: There is something you should know...

(GAIUS LUCIUS glares.)

ALFREDO: Marcus Benignus... *(He glances at MARCUS BENIGNUS, then whispers...)* Stole my ring.

(Beat)

GAIUS LUCIUS: So he *was* being punished.

ALFREDO: But it is strictly platonic.

GAIUS LUCIUS: Ahhhhhh... Please, please, forgive me.

ALFREDO: um...well...not right now.

GAIUS LUCIUS: Tonight maybe?

ALFREDO: You know where my tent is pitched?

GAIUS LUCIUS: What did you call me?!

ALFREDO: Pitched! Pitched!

GAIUS LUCIUS: Yes, Centurion, of course, Centurion.

ALFREDO: We will not speak of this again.

(*As they walk back over to* MARCUS BENIGNUS...)

GAIUS LUCIUS: I did not mean to suggest that there was anything socratic—

ALFREDO: Enough!

(*They rejoin* MARCUS BENIGNUS.)

ALFREDO: Now, you say you were frightened?

GAIUS LUCIUS: Yes, Centurion, he was horrible to behold.

MARCUS BENIGNUS: Visigoth?

GAIUS LUCIUS: More horrible than a Visigoth.

ALFREDO: Greek?

GAIUS LUCIUS: More horrible.

MARCUS BENIGNUS: What could be more horrible than a Greek?

GAIUS LUCIUS: If you could have seen him... (*Chomping and shaking his head like a dog with a chew toy:*) GNARR!

ALFREDO: So, Greek?

MARCUS BENIGNUS: We said Greek. Trojan?

GAIUS LUCIUS: He was like some kind of animal.

ALFREDO: Fish?

MARCUS BENIGNUS: Goat?

ALFREDO: Fish?

MARCUS BENIGNUS: Duck?

GAIUS LUCIUS: He had hair. All over his face. And fangs! Like a... Like a...

MARCUS BENIGNUS: ...furry ...serpent?

(Both of them glare at MARCUS BENIGNUS. *Then* GAIUS LUCIUS *turns angrily to* ALFREDO...)

GAIUS LUCIUS: How does he know about the furry serpent???

ALFREDO: It is not as it looks.

CABAL'S APARTMENT

*(*CABAL *is pacing.* BILL *and* BELLA *come in.* BILL *carries a bag of golf clubs.)*

CABAL: Bill! Bella!

BELLA: Cabal!

BILL: Cabal!

CABAL: What took you so long?

BELLA: Things got complicated.

CABAL: Things? What things?

BILL: Who wants to know?!

CABAL: Me, Bill. I want to know.

BILL: Cabal! Bella, it's Cabal.

CABAL: What things? What complications?

BELLA: The less we say about it, the better.

CABAL: Yes, of course. *(Pause)* But if you were to say—?

BELLA: We're not killers, Cabal! You know that.

CABAL: No, right, no, I didn't mean to imply—

BELLA: We clean hotel rooms. *That's it.* Right, Bill?

BILL: Maybe we do, maybe we don't.

CABAL: Right, that's right, you clean hotel rooms. And there's a certain...*hotel room* that needed...uh...cleaning.

BELLA: And you wannna know if we cleaned it?

CABAL: That's right.

(BELLA *and* BILL *confer in whispers.*)

BELLA: We cleaned it.

CABAL: Good.

BILL: Cleaned all of 'em.

CABAL: Good.

BILL: Right to the ground.

CABAL: Good. And what about the other room? The one at the hospital.

BILL: Sanitized for your protection.

CABAL: Excellent. So Piston's out of the picture permanently.

BILL: Yup.

BELLA: Not that we would know.

BILL: Nope.

CABAL: Perfect. Now no one will ever know what really happened at the Lakeview Hotel.

BILL: I know.

BELLA: No you don't.

BILL: I don't?

CABAL: No.

BILL: Does Bella?

BELLA: No.

CABAL: (*Waxing maniacal:*) Only I know the truth.

(*Taking the hint,* BILL *beats* CABAL *to death with a golf club.*)

BELLA: I don't think that's what she had in mind.

BILL: Oh.

FANTASY DICK'S OFFICE

FANTASY CHICK: Dick Piston...I need you...

FANTASY DICK: Yes...

FANTASY CHICK: I need your help.

FANTASY DICK: Is it the zipper?

FANTASY CHICK: No, it's not the Zipper. At least—
...I don't think that's his name.

FANTASY DICK: What *is* his name?

FANTASY CHICK: I'm not the detective here.

FANTASY DICK: And I'm not the steamy tart. But I guess
that was uncalled for.

FANTASY CHICK: I think I'm being watched.

FANTASY DICK: That goes without saying.

FANTASY CHICK: I have to know....

FANTASY DICK: What?

FANTASY CHICK: Who.

FANTASY DICK: Why?

FANTASY CHICK: Why what?

FANTASY DICK: Why who?

FANTASY CHICK: He seems to know my every move.
Where I am. What I think. How I feel.

FANTASY DICK: How do you feel?

(She takes his hands and places them on her body.)

FANTASY DICK: And this man...

FANTASY CHICK: Yes?

FANTASY DICK: *(Feeling her:)* He knows this?

FANTASY CHICK: Yes.

FANTASY DICK: I'll kill him. *(He draws his pistol and heads for the door.)*

FANTASY CHICK: Where are you doing?

FANTASY DICK: Where does any detective go at a time like this?

FANTASY CHICK: I don't know.

FANTASY DICK: Well, I'm pretty sure I leave the office.

FANTASY CHICK: Don't go. When you're here, I feel safe. And warm.

FANTASY DICK: When you're here I feel cheap and dirty. ...So we're both happy.

(He takes her in his arms and is about to kiss her, when...)

FANTASY DICK: Wait a minute.

FANTASY CHICK: What is it? What's wrong?

FANTASY DICK: You. Me. Here. Now. Why are we here?

FANTASY CHICK: There's a desk in here.

FANTASY DICK: No, listen to me. Piston's dead, he's gone. Why are we still here...unless...

(A door slams open, and PISTON enters in a trenchcoat and hat, trailing bandages, and looking like he's been through hell.)

PISTON: *(Gasping for breath:)* I'm back.

BLACKOUT

REVENGE
OF THE
INFINITE
CENTURION

EPISODE 10

"I've wasted another ten minutes and I'm no closer to
the solution than when I was dead."

CHARACTERS

DICK PISTON
CABBIE
HARLEQUIN
SHADOWY FIGURE
TODD MORTON
SPIKE
LARRY FINGERS
WOLFGANG BIEDERMANN
HERBERTO HERMOSA
HELGA HERMOSA
ALFREDO CENTAURI
MARCUS BENIGNUS

DICK PISTON

(Enter PISTON *with a notepad.)*

PISTON: The story I'm gonna tell you, yer not gonna believe. But every word of it is true. I know, because it happened to me. My name is Dick Piston, hotel detective. ...But we covered that. *(He flips ahead several pages in his notepad.)* The first time I died was bad. The second time was like something out of a storybook. A grisly *horrific* storybook with graphic descriptions of sadistic eroticism, that you keep on the top shelf so the kids won't get at it—Whoops whoops whoops. Waaaaaaaay ahead of myself. *(He flips back a few pages in his notepad.)* Cabal.

CABAL'S APARTMENT

PISTON: What brought me to the home of Cabal the hotel manager?

(Enter a cabdriver.)

CABBIE: Hey, man.

PISTON: Huh?

CABBIE: That's four fifty, man.

PISTON: Sorry, here you go.

*(*PISTON *pays the* CABBIE *who exits.)*

PISTON: Death has a way of clearing things up. My sinuses for one. And priorities. I knew now that solving this case was more than just a hobbie. More than a job.

More than an adventure. ...Whatever that would be. Call it love. Call it Ishmael, but I knew that at the end of this proverbial rainbow was a pot of gold that could suck the chrome off a set of hubcaps. One kiss told me that. And all I had to do was catch a killer.

(HARLEQUIN *appears...*)

HARLEQUIN: LARRY AND THE WEREWOLF. Episode Ten! (*...and vanishes.*)

PISTON: Herberto Hermosa was dead. Murdered. Snatched from the tender clutches of holy matrimony and torn into a half dozen bloody bite-size morsels. Why? Because that's what werewolves do. Wolfgang Biedermann was dead, too. Murdered by me when I discovered that he *was* that werewolf. Or so I thought. And Columbus thought he discovered India, but it don't make New York New Delhi. Y'see, lead bullets won't kill a werewolf. But that's what I pumped Biedermann full of after somebody removed the silver bullets from my gun. So Biedermann is an innocent man. ...Was an innocent man. ...No, he's *still* an innocent man. Just a dead one, that's all. Then there's me. Dick Piston, hotel detective. Trapped on the tenth floor of said hotel as it burned to the ground, I leaped to my death only to survive only to die at the hands of whoever's hands they were that were sent to murder me in my hospital bed. Cruel hands. Somewhat sticky hands. Hired hands in the employ of Cabal the hotel manager. Why? Because I was getting too close. Because Cabal didn't want me finding out what she already knew—that the werewolf who murdered Herberto Hermosa at the Lakeview Hotel still works at the Lakeview Hotel. Because Cabal the hotel manager *is* the werewolf! (*Then he notices* CABAL's *body.*) Damn. (*Pause*) Whoever stole the silver bullets from my gun must have known Cabal was a werewolf and used those bullets to... (*He looks at* CABAL *again.*) Wait, you

were bludgeoned. *(Pause)* Dammit, I've wasted another
ten minutes and I'm no closer to the solution than when
I was dead.

LARRY'S STUDIO

(A SHADOWY FIGURE *sits in a folding chair, waiting for the
show to begin.* TODD *comes in.)*

TODD: I just wanna thank you for coming again,
we're all, well, frankly, a little surprised. But pleasantly
surprised! And we're very sorry about what happened
last time. Very really very sorry. Really. But you won't
be, I promise you that. You will not be sorry. *(He leaves.
He comes back.)* ...that you came. *(He leaves.)*

LARRY FINGERS AND SPIKE

TODD: *(Voice over:)* Ladies and Gentlemen! Larry
Fingers aaaaaaaaaand Spike!

(Lights up on LARRY *and* SPIKE *onstage.* SPIKE *is very
intense.)*

SPIKE: *(Sings:)* When yer lyin' in a gutter.
Don't know which bread side is buttered
People passin' askin' "What're ya doin' here?"
*(The song is sung very rapidly, with long pauses between
stanzas where she seems to gather herself for the next phrase.)*
When yer drownin' all yer sorrows.
"What's today? There's no tomorrow."
Life's a bitch who runs a bar o-pen all night long.

(Pause. LARRY *vamps.)*

SPIKE: Then you hit the rocks at bottom
That's the breaks and you ain't got 'em
As at last yer askin' "What 'm I doin' here?"

(Pause)
So you stagger to a meeting
Stand in front, an' say the greeting
Spill yer guts of what's been eating you up inside.

Alcoholics Anonymous!
You save me from myself!
Alcoholics Anonymous!
Put the genie in the bottle,
Put the bottle on the she-elf!

Search your soul and did some steppin'.
Searched the box your soul was kep' in.
Faith said "leap", and so you lep' in. You don't ask
"How high?"

And you conquer what addicts you
Licked the liquor that afflicts you
Don't need spirits when your spirits needs a
picks-me-up.

Alcoholics Anonymous!
You put me back on track
Alcoholics Anonymous!
Rode the wagon, slayed the dragon
Got the monkey off my ba-ack

Alcoholics Anonymous!
You save me from myself!
Alcoholics Anonymous!
Put the genie in the bottle,
Put the bottle on the she-elf!

Say you're powerless to fight it?
I say, here's a bullet, bite it.
Get the lead out. Pull your head out.
Dug a hole? Y' gotta get out.

Alcoholics Anonymous!
From fire you pull my fat
Alcoholics Anonymous!

Kick some ass, and kick some habit.
Pull a rabbit from a ha-at.

Alcoholics Anonymous!
You save me from myself
Alcoholics Anonymous!
Put the genie in the bottle
Kick the habit. Ride the wagon.
Slayed the dragon. Spank the monkey. Pull the rabbit
off my back.
Put the genie-in-the-bottle and the monkey on the shelf!

My name is Spike.
And I'm an alcoholic.
(She raises her fist in triumph. End of song)

*(*TODD *enters applauding.)*

TODD: Fabulous, that was just fabulous. I just—
Look at me, I'm gushing.

SPIKE: Shut up, Todd. *(To* SHADOWY FIGURE:*)* Mister,
uh, sir, uh, this song is very personal to me, it deals
with stuff that, you know that's really personal stuff
that I have to deal with. And not because I'm a
necessarily an alcoholic. *(To* LARRY:*)* That's just a
metaphor, right Larry? But it's— Did you wanna
say something, Larry?

(As LARRY *is about to speak, the* SHADOWY FIGURE *pulls
out a gun and shoots him dead.)*

TODD: But...we have...other material.

HELGA'S LIVING ROOM

*(*HELGA *is anxiously waiting for a phone call.* BIEDERMANN
and HERMOSA *are also there, looking pretty bored. Finally,*
HELGA *can't take it anymore, she picks up the phone.)*

HERMOSA: Told ya she'd call him again!

BIEDERMANN: Wait. Maybe she's calling somebody else.

(HELGA *dials. The ghosts wait to see what she says.*
She says nothing.)

BIEDERMANN: Nope, it's him.

(BIEDERMANN *gives* HERMOSA *five bucks.* HELGA
continues to say nothing.)

HERMOSA: Kind of a one-sided conversation.

(HELGA *hangs up, frustrated, and exits.*)

HERMOSA: Maybe she's not getting through.

(BIEDERMANN *gets an idea...*)

BIEDERMANN: Oo! I know! *(He picks up the phone.)*

HERMOSA: What are you doing? Put that back.

BIEDERMANN: I'll hit redial and see who she's talking to.

HERMOSA: Stop it. You're acting like a fucking
poltergeist.

BIEDERMANN: Yeah, well, your wife is boring me to
death. *(He hits redial.)* Get it? Because I'm already dead?

HERMOSA: Yeah, you're a regular Bozo the Friendly
Ghost.

BIEDERMANN: It's just ringing.

HERMOSA: I told you! Now, put it down.

BIEDERMANN: One more ring.

HERMOSA: Put it down, she's coming back.

BIEDERMANN: Just a sec, just a sec.

HERMOSA: Here she comes!

(BIEDERMANN *slams the phone down and ducks behind*
some furniture, just as HELGA *enters.* HELGA *stops in the*
doorway, puzzled by what sounded like a slammed phone.)

HERMOSA: If we get exorcised, it's gonna be your fault.

BIEDERMANN: You could use the exorcise.

HERMOSA: Spook you!

BIEDERMANN: Haunt this!

(HELGA *shrugs, goes to the phone and dials the number again. Pause*)

HELGA & BIEDERMANN: Why doesn't he answer?

(HELGA *hangs up, perplexed.*)

HERMOSA: *(Hypnotically:)* Gooooo to him, Helga...

BIEDERMANN: Oh! Good idea! *(Hypnotically:)* Goooooo, Helga... Goooo...

(HELGA *looks like she needs to pee.*)

HERMOSA: To him! To *himmmmm...*

BIEDERMANN: Oops. Sorry.

HELGA: Maybe I should go to him.

(*The ghosts high five each other.*)

HELGA: Maybe he's in trouble! Maybe he needs my help! He could be injured. He could be trapped under some heavy equipment, and needs someone with super human strength to get him out! *(She runs out, but then comes back.)* Oh. I don't *have* super human strength.

BIEDERMANN: We were so close.

HELGA: But, wait, I'm a nurse! A registered nurse! If he's injured, I can tend his wounds until someone with superhuman strength comes along! *(She dashes out.)*

ALFREDO'S APARTMENT

(MARCUS BENIGNUS *comes in just as* ALFREDO *is about to sneak out the front door.*)

MARCUS BENIGNUS: Where are you going?

ALFREDO: (*Evasively:*) I need to meditate.

MARCUS BENIGNUS: There's a karmic balance here. You don't need to go out.

ALFREDO: Where I free my mind, is my own business, Marcus.

MARCUS BENIGNUS: You're going to see her, aren't you?

(ALFREDO *stops in his tracks.*)

MARCUS BENIGNUS: You're not the only one with heightened perceptions acquired through years of zen training, Alfredus.

ALFREDO: Jealousy clouds your judgement, Marcus. I go to see him.

MARCUS BENIGNUS: Jealousy clouds yours or you would kill him and end this ceaseless stalking.

ALFREDO: I have a far, far greater revenge planned for him.

MARCUS BENIGNUS: What? What is your plan?

ALFREDO: You will know soon enough.

MARCUS BENIGNUS: When? When will I know? When will it happen?! When can we get this over with and go back to living a normal life?!

(*Beat.* ALFREDO *glares.*)

ALFREDO: *We* will never have a normal life, Marcus. *This* is not normal.

(ALFREDO *exits.* MARCUS BENIGNUS *goes to the door and shouts after him...*)

MARCUS BENIGNUS: Fine! Have it your way! Delay the inevitable. Drag it out. Keep us all in suspense.

(*Suddenly,* ALFREDO *is in the doorway again, startling* MARCUS BENIGNUS.)

ALFREDO: ...Perhaps I will.

LARRY'S STUDIO

(LARRY *is dead on the floor.*)

SPIKE: Larry, speak to me! Speak to me!!

TODD: Spike! Spike! He can't hear you!

SPIKE: You mean...? He's dead?

TODD: I mean, he's got his ear plugs in. (*He takes* LARRY's *earplugs out.*) There. *Now* he can't hear you 'cause he's dead.

SPIKE: We've got to call 9-1-1. (*She runs to the phone, picks it up.*) The phone's dead, too! He cut the phone line!

TODD: He didn't cut the phone line. It's unplugged so it wouldn't ring during the audition. (*He plugs the phone back in.*)

SPIKE: A dial tone! There's a dial tone! (*She dials 9-1-1.*) Hello! 9-1-1? This is an emergency! Yes, an emergency! ...What's my name? (*She hangs up. To* TODD:) You have to call them.

TODD: What? Why?

SPIKE: Just call them.

TODD: But you're right there.

SPIKE: (*Murderously:*) Just get over here and call them, before I do something I might regret in *two* states.

(TODD *goes to the phone and dials 911.*)

TODD: Hi! This is Todd Morton— ...No, I don't mind holding.

SPIKE: I've got to go, Larry. You know why. But I want you to know that... even though I never said it before... you know how I feel.

TODD: *(On phone:)* Yes, hi, is this gonna take long? We've got kind of an emergency here. A man's been shot. Yeah, shot dead. Yes, completely dead. How dead does he have to be? He's dead. Oh, I see you're point.... Okay, sure, you take your time, we're not in any immediate danger— Agh!!

(SPIKE *smashes a guitar over* TODD's *head. Just then* BIEDERMANN *and* HERMOSA *burst in.*)

HERMOSA: Wooo!

(HELGA *can be heard clambering up the stairs behind them.*)

BIEDERMANN: *(To* HERMOSA:) Are you sure this is where she's going?

HERMOSA: I guess.

BIEDERMANN: *(Looking back out the door:)* What is she doing?

HERMOSA: *(Shouting out the door to* HELGA:) I told you not to run on stairs! ...In heels! ...With tools!

BIEDERMANN: Boy, she sure got dressed up for this.

HERMOSA: I'm not jealous.

(BIEDERMANN *notices that the phone is off the hook.*)

BIEDERMANN: Well, here's the problem. The phone was off the hook.

HERMOSA: Hmm.

(BIEDERMANN *notices* SPIKE.)

BIEDERMANN: Who's the pirate? She's hot!

(HELGA *bursts through the door, in stunning formal attire, and with a crowbar.*)

HELGA: Larry???

SPIKE: What are you doing here?

HELGA: I'm a nurse. And I brought a crowbar. Where is he?

SPIKE: *(To herself:)* That was quick.

(HELGA *sees* LARRY, *throws herself across his body.*)

HELGA: Larry! Larry speak to me!

BIEDERMANN: *(To* HERMOSA:*)* Who's the dead guy?

HERMOSA: That's him!! That's the guy who killed me!

BLACKOUT

EPISODE 11

"Cute. For a murderer..."

CHARACTERS

HARLEQUIN
ALFREDO CENTAURI
MARCUS BENIGNUS
GAIUS LUCIUS
THE WEREWOLF
FANTASY DICK
FANTASY CHICK
DICK PISTON
HELGA HERMOSA
WOLFGANG BIEDERMANN
HERBERTO HERMOSA

HARLEQUIN

HARLEQUIN: LARRY AND THE WEREWOLF. Episode
Eleven! Awooooo...

ROME—TWELVE B.C.

(ALFREDO *and* MARCUS BENIGNUS *are standing watch.*
GAIUS LUCIUS *approaches them.*)

ALFREDO: Have you anything to report?

(GAIUS LUCIUS *says nothing, but hands him a scroll.*)

MARCUS BENIGNUS: Hail, Gaius Lucius.

(GAIUS LUCIUS *ignores him.*)

MARCUS BENIGNUS: Gaius Lucius?

(GAIUS LUCIUS *still says nothing.*)

MARCUS BENIGNUS: I think Gaius Lucius is angry with
us, Centurion. Look how quiet he is. Never speaks.
Submits his reports in writing. Won't even look us
in the eye. I wonder why that is. I wonder what could
be gnawing at him. Gnawing at him like an insect.
Like a great jealous insect who's lost his favorite piece
of wood, and shall never have it again, because it
belongs to someone else now, and he shall never have
it again! (*He affectionately snuggles up to* ALFREDO.)
Don't you, Centurion?

ALFREDO: Enough! Some unholy thing has unleashed
its demon upon the Roman countryside and you can

only bicker like two she-bitches deprived of a single piece of meat.

(MARCUS BENIGNUS *is abashed.* GAIUS LUCIUS *just glares.*)

ALFREDO: I could understand if you blamed the piece of meat. It is delicious and fickle. But why quarrel with one another? You are alike in this. You should be friends. Allies.

MARCUS BENIGNUS: Yes, Centurion.

(GAIUS LUCIUS *just glares.*)

ALFREDO: Come, make your peace with one another.

(*Pause*)

MARCUS BENIGNUS: Gaius Lucius, I am sorry if I have offended thee.

(MARCUS BENIGNUS *offers his hand.* GAIUS LUCIUS *shakes his hand.*)

ALFREDO: Well, this is cold friendship. Embrace each other! You are brothers, you are Romans!

(MARCUS BENIGNUS *and* GAIUS LUCIUS *embrace.*)

ALFREDO: Somehow I doubt your sincerity.

(*Sullen silence.* MARCUS BENIGNUS *kisses* GAIUS LUCIUS. ALFREDO *smiles lasciviously.*)

ALFREDO: Somehow I *still* doubt your sincerity.

(GAIUS LUCIUS *glares.* MARCUS BENIGNUS *swallows hard.* MARCUS BENIGNUS *starts to remove his tunic. But* GAIUS LUCIUS, *enraged, draws a sword and attacks him.* MARCUS BENIGNUS *tries to defend himself, but he is quickly overpowered, and falls to the ground.* ALFREDO *does nothing.* GAIUS LUCIUS *is about to finish* MARCUS BENIGNUS *off when... The* WEREWOLF *springs in from out of nowhere! It barrels into* GAIUS LUCIUS *hurling him away. It then turns to pounce on* MARCUS BENIGNUS *itself.*

ALFREDO *tries to pull the* WEREWOLF *off of the helpless*
MARCUS BENIGNUS, *but it flings him back with a shrug,*
rips MARCUS BENIGNUS *open and devours his heart. As*
the WEREWOLF *rises from the dead body,* GAIUS LUCIUS
charges in, and impales it with a sword. The WEREWOLF
disembowels GAIUS LUCIUS *and pulls the sword out of itself*
just in time to parry an attack from ALFREDO. ALFREDO
and the WEREWOLF *duel briefly. They grab each other's*
wrists and seem for a moment to be at an impasse. But the
WEREWOLF *pulls* ALFREDO *toward it and drives its fangs*
into his throat. As ALFREDO *slumps to the ground, the*
WEREWOLF *howls, victorious.)*

FANTASY

(FANTASY CHICK *screams.)*

FANTASY CHICK: No, no, no, stay away, get away!
Nooooo!

FANTASY DICK: ...And then what?

FANTASY CHICK: That's it. Then I came here.

FANTASY DICK: I see.

FANTASY CHICK: Do you?

FANTASY DICK: Not at all.

FANTASY CHICK: I see.

(*He turns to the audience...)*

FANTASY DICK: Her story left a lot to the imagination.
Like a one minute call to a 900 number. There was
more to this girl than meets the eye. But in that dress...
Not much more.

(*He turns again to her...)*

FANTASY DICK: Can you think of anyone who might
want to hurt you?

FANTASY CHICK: In a good way?

FANTASY DICK: In the usual way. An old boyfriend maybe?

FANTASY CHICK: Only these. (*She takes out a stack of photographs.*)

FANTASY DICK: You came prepared.

(*She hands him a photo.*)

FANTASY CHICK: This is Mario. My first. It ended very badly.

FANTASY DICK: So he could be the one.

FANTASY CHICK: I don't see how. Mario's dead.

FANTASY DICK: So it ended *very* badly.

FANTASY CHICK: He was murdered by Tony.

(*She hands him another photo.*)

FANTASY DICK: Cute. For a murderer.

FANTASY CHICK: That's what first drew me to him.

FANTASY DICK: And...?

FANTASY CHICK: It ended very badly. This is Patrick, my boyfriend after Tony.

(*She hands him another photo.*)

FANTASY DICK: How did this one end?

(*She hands him another photo.*)

FANTASY CHICK: This is Guido.

FANTASY DICK: Patrick didn't stand much of a chance.

FANTASY CHICK: It was quick and painless, if that's what you mean.

FANTASY DICK: And who killed Guido?

FANTASY CHICK: Guido's alive.

FANTASY DICK: Then he might be the one.

FANTASY CHICK: You wouldn't say that if you saw him today.

FANTASY DICK: He's a changed man?

FANTASY CHICK: He's a triple amputee. This is Nickie.

(*She hands him another photo.*)

FANTASY DICK: You've got a lot of nude pictures of yourself.

FANTASY CHICK: Would you believe we were lovers if we were fully dressed at a shoe store in the mall?

FANTASY DICK: That's a shoe store?

(*She hands him another photo.*)

FANTASY CHICK: This is the—

FANTASY DICK: I *recognize* the president.

FANTASY CHICK: *He's* still alive.

(FANTASY DICK *points at something in one of the photos.*)

FANTASY DICK: Waitaminute, who's *this* guy?

FANTASY CHICK: The bellhop?

FANTASY DICK: Yes. He's in every picture. Lurking in the background. Look, here he's the news vendor. Traffic cop. Third base coach. And here he's the rodeo clown.

FANTASY CHICK: That's my pimp.

FANTASY DICK: Pimp? You mean...?

FANTASY CHICK: It's just a hobby.

FANTASY DICK: With this kind of talent you oughta think about entering a craft show.

FANTASY CHICK: You think I have talent?

FANTASY DICK: I never thought I'd call it that, but yes.

FANTASY CHICK: That's the kindest thing anyone's ever said to me.

FANTASY DICK: I wanna talk to this bellhop.

(*She kisses him passionately.*)

FANTASY CHICK: Forget about the bellhop.

FANTASY DICK: The who?

(*With a gasp, the real* PISTON *wakes from a dream.*)

PISTON: The bellhop! That's who I'm forgetting!

OUTSIDE ALFREDO'S APARTMENT

(*As* ALFREDO *leaves his apartment, he encounters* HELGA *coming to see him.*)

ALFREDO: I knew you'd come back to me.

(HELGA *lunges at him. He pulls her into his arms.*)

ALFREDO: You are mine.

HELGA: I'm not yours. I was never yours. I will never be yours. I have never been going to be yours!

ALFREDO: You say that now...

HELGA: And after what you've done to Larry, I will never be going to have been going to be yours!

ALFREDO: What I've done to Larry Fingers is only just beginning, Mrs Hermosa.

HELGA: You killed him! What else are you going to do?

ALFREDO: What?? He's dead?! NO!

(ALFREDO *dashes out.* HELGA *is left bewildered.*)

HERMOSA: (*To* BIEDERMANN:) I say we haunt *him* instead.

BIEDERMANN: He's hot.

HERMOSA & BIEDERMANN: *(Running off:)* Woooo!

BLACKOUT

EPISODE 12

"Show him your ninja stuff, Bella."

CHARACTERS

HARLEQUIN
DICK PISTON
BILL BOLA
BELLA BOLA
ALFREDO CENTAURI
WOLFGANG BIEDERMANN
HERBERTO HERMOSA
GAIUS LUCIUS
SPIKE
LARRY FINGERS

HARLEQUIN

HARLEQUIN: LARRY AND THE WEREWOLF. Episode Twelve! Awooooo...

THE HOME OF BILL & BELLA BOLA

(Enter PISTON.*)*

PISTON: The home of Bill and Bella Bola. The bellhops. The proverbial butlers, if you will. The proverbial trees for which I could not see the forest. Or maybe they were the forest. That one's always confused me. But one thing was as plain as the nose on my proverbial face... Oh my God! *(Then, he finds his nose.)* Oh. There it is.

BELLA: *(Offstage:)* Bill?

PISTON: With so many obvious suspects, I'd overlooked the obvious. That something really really *weird* was going on. Something so convoluted and sinister, that only one word could describe it... *Convolinister*—! No... *(Takes a moment to remember the right word)* Conspiracy!

BILL: *(Also offstage:)* Bella?

PISTON: It was just a theory, but a quick phone call to the police confirmed that Bill and Bella Bola were *not* wanted in connection with hundreds of unsolved murders. Murders they apparently had not committed. Murders they *could* not have committed. And that was all the proof I needed. You see, Belladonna Bola and her brother Bilbo were no mere bellhops. They were killers. Assassins. Professional hitmen and women with a particular penchant for preventing police detection. But they were up against a different kind of detection this time. They were up against me...

BILL: *(Entering:)* Dick Piston, hotel detective!

PISTON: And erotic novelist.

(BELLA enters.)

BELLA: Piston!

PISTON: *(Barks:)* I'll ask the questions, if you don't mind! *(Realizes he spoke out of turn:)* Sorry, didn't mean to interrupt.

BELLA: Piston! What are you doing here?

PISTON: *(Barks:)* I'll ask the questions, if you don't mind! I know all about you and your brother, Bella.

BILL: My name's Bill.

BELLA: Yeah, I'm Bella.

PISTON: I know all about you and your brother Bill, Bella.

BILL: Bill *Bola.*

PISTON: Shut up! I know all about you! Bella Bola— ex-Navy Seal, Green Beret and Mafia hitwoman.

BELLA: Hitman. Don't patronize me, Piston.

BILL: And she's a ninja. Show him your ninja stuff, Bella.

PISTON: And you. Bill Bola—two bit thug.

BILL: With a capital two.

PISTON: The two of you are the ones behind the conspiracy at the Lakeview Hotel. You're the brains, and you're the muscle.

BELLA: You're wrong about us, Piston.

PISTON: Wrong about your involvement in the attempt to make Herberto Hermosa's grisly murder look like a grisly suicide?

BELLA: No, you're right there.

PISTON: Wrong about your connection to the destruction of the Lakeview Hotel?

BELLA: Nope.

PISTON: Wrong about you having a hand in the homicide of the hotel manager Cabal, and myself?

BILL: So we *did* kill you. Then how—?

(BELLA *glares at* BILL.)

BELLA: No, you got me there, too, Piston.

PISTON: So what am I wrong about?

BELLA: *(Pointing at* BILL:) *He's* the brains!! Look out!

(BELLA *ducks.* PISTON *turns to deflect* BILL's *attack, but* BILL *is just standing there.* BILL *shrugs. While* PISTON *is distracted,* BELLA *breaks a vase over his head, knocking him out.)*

LARRY'S STUDIO

(LARRY's *body is still lying on the floor when* ALFREDO *rushes in.)*

ALFREDO: Fingers!

(BIEDERMANN *and* HERMOSA *also rush in.)*

BIEDERMANN: Agh! We're back here again.

HERMOSA: That's him!! That's the guy who killed me!

BIEDERMANN: Oh, shut up.

(A SHADOWY FIGURE emerges from the shadows with a gun. The SHADOWY FIGURE removes his shadowy hat, revealing himself to be GAIUS LUCIUS the THIRD CENTURION.)

ALFREDO: You!

GAIUS LUCIUS: Yes.

ALFREDO: Why?

GAIUS LUCIUS: Because.

ALFREDO: Because why?

GAIUS LUCIUS: Just because.

ALFREDO: There's something you're not telling me.

GAIUS LUCIUS: Ooo! Those heightened perceptions! They just give me chills!

ALFREDO: Stop it.

GAIUS LUCIUS: I'm thinking of a number.

ALFREDO: Sixty-nine. Tell me why you have done this.

GAIUS LUCIUS: What? Killed Larry Fingers. No reason. Random act of violence.

ALFREDO: He was mine!

GAIUS LUCIUS: Yes, he was! How unsatisfied you must be.

ALFREDO: I demand an explanation.

GAIUS LUCIUS: You are too slow, Alfredus. Zen training has made you weak.

ALFREDO: My vengeance is like a dagger.

GAIUS LUCIUS: Mine is like a bomb!!

ALFREDO: Is that what this is about?

GAIUS LUCIUS: I dunno, is it? *(He thinks of a number.)*

ALFREDO: Sixty-nine. You should have stayed at the monastery. Learned to harness your rage. You don't have to become the wolf.

GAIUS LUCIUS: I want to become the wolf! I like the wolf! Your way is not my way, Alfredus. Those years in the monastery, learning to control our passions, were torture for me. ...But you knew that. You relished my suffering in that boring Buddhist purgatory.

ALFREDO: I'm sorry you think so.

GAIUS LUCIUS: Are you sorry you've done so, Alfredus?! Or is remorse another emotion you pretend not to feel? As it tears at your insides like an intestinal jackal. You may have fooled the monks, Alfredus, but I know you. Your placid exterior is merely the soft fluffy surface of a roiling storm cloud. Your delicate inner peace is a bubble about to burst. A twig about to snap. A tectonic plate about to slide into the ocean taking all of California with it!

ALFREDO: What did Larry Fingers do to you?

GAIUS LUCIUS: Nothing.

ALFREDO: This is not about nothing!!

GAIUS LUCIUS: This is exactly about nothing, Alfredus. None of this—*all of this*—none of it had to happen. *(Pause)* Do you remember the werewolf?

ALFREDO: The one that bit us?

GAIUS LUCIUS: The one that disemboweled us! The one that, had you not hounded him like a dog, might have let us live out our natural days growing old and fat in the imperial Roman Senate. But you hunted him like an animal.

ALFREDO: He *was* an animal.

GAIUS LUCIUS: And like an animal, when cornered, he ripped your guts out. Still you pursued him. Across

Europe, and half of Asia. For five hundred years you stalked him. Although, in those days it was called courting.

ALFREDO: I did not—! ...You say that just to rile me.

GAIUS LUCIUS: You know me too well. *(He thinks of a number.)*

ALFREDO: Sixty-nine. Yes, I followed him for five hundred years, until one night in Beijing, he could take it no more, and committed suicide with silver bullets he had made by hand. One of the first lethal uses of Chinese gunpowder. *(He chuckles.)* How he must have suffered. *(He chuckles again.)* It's true what they say. Revenge is a cold, sweet dish. Like ice cream. *(He laughs out loud.)* I only wish I could have been there.

GAIUS LUCIUS: There really wasn't much to see.

(ALFREDO stops laughing.)

ALFREDO: You were there?

GAIUS LUCIUS: There was a party, of course. He loved to party. Rice wine spritzers and opium brownies. And then we got to talking about you. And laughing. After I explained who you were, that is. He had no idea. You pursued him across two continents, Alfredus, *because he liked to travel*. He didn't know you were behind him the whole way. Trying to keep up. For five centuries, you matched wits with one man's busy social calendar. You were not his nemesis, you were his groupie. *(He chuckles.)* I told him your story and he laughed and laughed. He laughed his head off. And then I blew his head off. That's how he died. Drunk and happy. And at my hands. I only wish you could have been there.... Ten minutes too late. Like you are now.

(ALFREDO seethes.)

GAIUS LUCIUS: I killed Larry Fingers, Alfredus, because you hate him. You loathe him, and you have devoted your life to making him suffer as no man has ever suffered. ...And I've taken that away from you. I think I shall kill everyone you hate. Everyone who gives your life meaning. While you meditate on revenge, I shall exact it for you. I get to have all the fun, and you get to have all the focus.

(GAIUS LUCIUS *laughs.* ALFREDO *takes a step toward him.*)

GAIUS LUCIUS: Ah! Careful, Alfredus. I can take my revenge fast *or* slow. And these are silver bullets.

ALFREDO: *(Calling his bluff:)* You wouldn't kill me.

GAIUS LUCIUS: No, of course not! I wouldn't kill you! I wouldn't murder those monks. I wouldn't eat that virgin. I wouldn't infect Europe with the plague just to spoil your Mardi Gras plans.

ALFREDO: You monster!

GAIUS LUCIUS: Takes one to know one.

(ALFREDO *tries to control his fury.*)

GAIUS LUCIUS: That's right, Alfredus, don't wolf out on me now. Remember your allergies.

(ALFREDO *regains his composure.*)

GAIUS LUCIUS: You know, I was going to drag this out. Make you suffer. But I just don't have your patience. And you'll probably never be this angry again. In fact... I can guarantee it. *(He puts his gun to* ALFREDO's *head. With a grin:)* Goodbye, Alfredus. I'll give Marcus Benignus your love. Twice, if he has the stamina.

ALFREDO: Rrrrr...!

(*Just then,* SPIKE *bursts into the room with a pistol and guns* GAIUS LUCIUS *down.*)

SPIKE: *(To* ALFREDO:*)* I don't know who you are, Mister, but I had to kill him. I had to. That's the man who shot Larry. *(Sob)* And now they're both dead.

*(*ALFREDO *goes to* GAIUS LUCIUS's *body, and takes* GAIUS LUCIUS's *gun.)*

ALFREDO: You didn't use silver bullets. *(He shoots* GAIUS LUCIUS *several times.)* Now, they're both dead.

(Just then, LARRY *sits up.)*

SPIKE: Larry!

ALFREDO: Fingers!

(In a panic, ALFREDO *whirls and shoots* LARRY, *too.)*

SPIKE: No!

*(*SPIKE *shoots* ALFREDO. *When the smoke clears,* LARRY, ALFREDO *and* GAIUS LUCIUS *are all dead on the floor.* SPIKE *faints.)*

HERMOSA: Wow.

BIEDERMANN: You know, it was kinda talky there for awhile, but that end was *so exciting!*

BILL & BELLA'S BASEMENT

*(*PISTON *is tied to a chair in the* BOLA *basement.* BILL *and* BELLA *in black leather S & M garb with whips and other instruments of erotic torture.)*

BELLA: All right, Piston, now *we*'ll be asking the questions. *(To* BILL:*)* Anything you wanna know, Bill?

BILL: Where'd he get that hat?

BELLA: I'm not gonna ask him about the hat! *(To* PISTON:*)* That is a nice one, though, where'd you get it?

PISTON: I'm not talking to you.

BILL: And how come he's not dead?

BELLA: Oh, good one. (*To* PISTON:) How'd ya do that?

PISTON: You wouldn't believe me if I told you.

BELLA: Oh, I don't know. Me and Bill's pretty gullible. Aren't we, Bill?

BILL: Is that a trick question?

PISTON: You'll never get away with this!

BILL: Bella! He knows about *this*!

(BELLA *elbows* BILL *to shut him up.*)

BELLA: With what, exactly? I need you to be more specific.

PISTON: What??

BELLA: I don't think you know who you're dealing with Piston.

PISTON: Oh, I think I do.

BELLA: Yeah, that's what Bill says, too.

BILL: Yer pretty smart.

BELLA: So, I gotta know. Who do you think you're dealing with?

PISTON: A two-bit crook, and her two-bit brother.

BELLA: So fifty cents for the both of us? You underestimate me, Piston.

PISTON: And you underestimate me.

BILL: You underestimated us, first!

BELLA: Bill! Quiet! (*To* PISTON:) Piston, you seem to think you know a lot about us. But, if you know what you say you think you know, then you know we can't have just anybody runnin' around knowing what you say you know about us. Y'know what I mean? ...And if you don't know what I mean... Well, maybe we should pretend we never had this conversation, okay?

PISTON: What do you want from me?

BELLA: Only everything, Piston. I want you to start at the beginning. And tell me everything.

PISTON: The whole story?

BELLA: The whole story.

PISTON: Buy the book!

(BILL *thinks that's funny.* BELLA *glares at him.*)

BELLA: So that's the way it's gonna be?

PISTON: Yeah, it's gonna be that way.

BELLA: All right, Piston, you leave me no choice.

(BILL *hands* BELLA *a whip.*)

PISTON: Do your worst.

BELLA: I appreciate the offer, Piston, but since this is your first time, I think we should start off easy, and work up to my worst. Don't ya think?

PISTON: Get on with it, Bella. You don't scare me. I've been dead once today. There's nothing you and your brother can do that will—ugh!

(BILL *and* BELLA *are kissing and fondling each other.*)

PISTON: No. Oh, God, no! NO!!!!

BLACKOUT

EPISODE 13

"You're alive! Again!"

CHARACTERS

HARLEQUIN
HERBERTO HERMOSA
WOLFGANG BIEDERMANN
ALFREDO CENTAURI
LARRY FINGERS
GAIUS LUCIUS
SPIKE
TODD MORTON
DICK PISTON
FANTASY DICK
FANTASY CHICK
BILL BOLA
BELLA BOLA

HARLEQUIN

HARLEQUIN: LARRY AND THE WEREWOLF. Episode Thirteen! Awooooo...

LARRY'S STUDIO

(The bodies of LARRY, ALFREDO *and* GAIUS LUCIUS *lie on the floor.* BIEDERMANN *and* HERMOSA *are sulking nearby.)*

HERMOSA: You realize we're out of work again.

BIEDERMANN: Y'know, this is fun, but I think we gotta haunt someone in the service industry.

HERMOSA: Or textiles. Something with a lower mortality rate

BIEDERMANN: Yeah! Maybe something health-related.

HERMOSA: Well, we had a nurse.

BIEDERMANN: I was thinking, like, an aerobics instructor.

HERMOSA: I just wish we haunted someone who could see us. I mean, what's the point of being all ghostly, if no one knows you're here? Hey, wanna see me levitate?

(Just then, ALFREDO *sits up, startling the ghosts.)*

BIEDERMANN & HERMOSA: Agh!!

BIEDERMANN: *(To* ALFREDO:*)* You scared the bejeezus outta me!

HERMOSA: He can't hear us.

BIEDERMANN: Y'know, that's another thing. We gotta haunt someone who can hear us.

HERMOSA: Yeah, like maybe a *psychic* aerobics instructor.

BIEDERMANN: Except then she might be self-conscious about aerobercizing in front of us. We don't want that.

HERMOSA: Why do you assume she'll be a she?

BIEDERMANN: Because if we're just gonna haunt a guy, we might as well find someone like Piston.

(*The ghosts get a little choked up.*)

HERMOSA: Piston. I miss him.

BIEDERMANN: The way his face would get all red. (*He sniffles.*)

HERMOSA: Come on, buddy. Piston's gone to a better place. A place without pain. Without hate.

BIEDERMANN: And chock full of hot chicks.

HERMOSA: Oh, stop it. It's not full of hot chicks.

BIEDERMANN: Well, then what makes it better?

(ALFREDO *gets up and exits.*)

HERMOSA: Say, how's he doing that? Shouldn't he be dead?

HERMOSA: You really weren't paying attention, were you?

BIEDERMANN: Once they start talkin', I just zone out.

HERMOSA: That guy's a werewolf. You gotta shoot him with silver bullets.

(LARRY *sits up.*)

BIEDERMANN: Agh! Larry's a werewolf, too!

HERMOSA: I never suspected.

BIEDERMANN: But wait, didn't he get shot with silver bullets?

HERMOSA: We better ask him.

BIEDERMANN & HERMOSA: Mister Fingers! Mister Fingers! Woo!

(*But* LARRY *exits without noticing them.*)

BIEDERMANN: I'm tellin' ya, a psychic aerobics instructor.

HERMOSA: So does this mean the other one's not dead, either?

BIEDERMANN: I don't see how. They shot him with both kinds of bullets.

HERMOSA: Five bucks says the other one gets up, too.

BIEDERMANN: Yer on!

(*They gather over* GAIUS LUCIUS's *body.*)

BIEDERMANN: Stay down! Stay down!

HERMOSA: Come on, poppa needs a new set o' sheets!

(GAIUS LUCIUS *sits up.*)

HERMOSA:	BIEDERMANN:
Yes!!	No!!

(BIEDERMANN *gives* HERMOSA *five bucks.*)

HERMOSA: Ten bucks says he can't hear us.

(*They stare at* GAIUS LUCIUS, *expectantly.*)

GAIUS LUCIUS: Fuck off.

HERMOSA:	BIEDERMANN:
No!!	Yes!!

HERMOSA: Waitaminute, he just told us to fuck off.

(GAIUS LUCIUS *starts to leave, and they run after him.*)

BIEDERMANN: Hey, Mister! Mister! We're sorry to bother you, but you don't mind if we haunt you, do ya? Most people can't hear us. Woo!

(GAIUS LUCIUS *punches* BIEDERMANN *in the nose.*)

GAIUS LUCIUS: Most people aren't dead.

HERMOSA: Feisty.

BIEDERMANN: He broke my nose.

HERMOSA: Hey, so you're a ghost? You wanna hang out with us? Roam the earth. Haunt the living. Best seats at the Stones concert.

GAIUS LUCIUS: I roamed the earth for two thousand years. I'm going to hell where I can get some rest. (*He departs.*)

BIEDERMANN: He's kind of a bitch.

SPIKE

(SPIKE *sings an a cappella number.*)

SPIKE: Whispers of lipstick
She drops him a glance
The motor is running
There's no time to dance
She slips into shadows
He slips in a trance
The clock striking twelve
Splits the end of their chance

And they all away
And they all saunter home
And they all away into the night.

(TODD *has come in and, finding* SPIKE *singing alone, goes to* SPIKE's *piano and plays her accompaniment as she continues.*)

SPIKE: He sits in the pub
And he worships the ground
She treads underfoot
As she waltzes around
And scribbles his love
On the back of a pound
She slips in her garter
As he buys the next round

And they all away
And they all saunter home
And they all away into the night.

(LARRY *comes in.* SPIKE *lets out a little gasp.* LARRY *glares at* TODD, *who stops playing and slowly backs away from the piano.)*

THE BOLA BASEMENT

(PISTON, *unconscious, is still tied to a chair.* HARLEQUIN *appears from behind the chair, dressed like* PISTON. *He takes* PISTON's *hat to complete the costume.* HARLEQUIN *does his best* PISTON *impression...)*

HARLEQUIN: I used to have a friend who used to tell me...

FANTASY

(FANTASY DICK *enters wearing a bathrobe.)*

FANTASY DICK: I used to have a friend who used to tell me "Quit while you're ahead, Piston. Quit while you're ahead." And on that fateful Friday night I was one great big enormous head. The girl of my dreams had walked into my life shattering the illusion that dreams don't come true. An illusion I never much liked in the first place. I wanted her. She needed me. And between the two of us, we were almost fully dressed. It was like some warped adolescent fantasy. Of course, there had to be a catch. When she walked into my office like something out of a sticky dream sequence in a dimly lit play, a mystery walked in right behind her. Not exactly behind her. More like beside her. No, more like she was wearing it. Mystery was wrapped all around her like skin tight edible lingerie. And my job was to peel her out of it, without choking on the fabric. And that was the catch. Because rule number one in this business is don't put your mouth on the client. *(He takes a moment to light a cigarette.)* I knew I was in too deep when I saw her in scuba gear.

(FANTASY CHICK walks in wearing a skin-tight rubber outfit.)

FANTASY DICK: I used to have a friend who used to tell me, "Never sleep on the buttered side of your bread." He was drunk as hell at the time, but he said it.

(FANTASY CHICK slinks toward FANTASY DICK.)

FANTASY DICK: *(To FANTASY CHICK:)* I'm gonna tell you something I've never said to a woman in rubber before. ...No.

FANTASY CHICK: I don't know the meaning of the word.

(She tries to kiss him.)

FANTASY DICK: Then here's another one. Down, girl.

(She starts to go down on him. He has to stop her.)

FANTASY DICK: Let me be blunt.

FANTASY CHICK: Like an instrument?

FANTASY DICK: Listen, this is no good. You're a hot tomato, baby. But you're a hot potato, too.

FANTASY CHICK: You sure know how to make a girl feel all edible.

FANTASY DICK: I just don't wanna burn my tongue.

FANTASY CHICK: Then maybe you should keep your tongue in your pants.

FANTASY DICK: That's what I'm sayin', but you ain't listening.

FANTASY CHICK: I'm sorry, English is my second language.

FANTASY DICK: What's your first?

FANTASY CHICK: Body language.

(He slaps her. She kisses him. He pushes her away. She rips open his shirt. He kisses her. She slaps him.)

FANTASY DICK: But I don't want to get into a long drawn-out discussion.

(As she unzips the front of her wet suit, FANTASY DICK tries to back away from her.)

FANTASY DICK: There's something not right about this. Call it deja vu. Call it too many scotch martinis. But somehow I get the feeling we've done this before.

FANTASY CHICK: We have, Dick. ...I'm your little sister.

(She pulls open her wetsuit, exposing her chest to him.)

FANTASY DICK: Oh God! No!!

THE BOLA BASEMENT

PISTON: *(Waking up:)* Oh God! No!!

(But there's nobody there. Then BILL and BELLA come in wearing bathrobes and smoking cigarettes.)

PISTON: You monsters! I don't care what you do. I'm not telling you nothing!

BELLA: You already did.

PISTON: I did?

BILL: What a wimp.

BELLA: You told us everything. You held nothing back. You spilled your guts, your beans.

BILL: Your cat.

(BELLA *raises an eyebrow at* BILL.)

BILL: From the bag.

BELLA: You told us your whole story, Piston. And we don't believe it.

PISTON: But every word is true!

BELLA: Well, we don't believe it!!

(BILL *raises his hand.*)

BELLA: All right, Bill believes it. But I don't.

(BILL *gives* BELLA *a look.*)

BELLA: All right, I believe it, too. But if you tell anyone we believed your cockamamie story about coming back from the grave to catch a werewolf and find your fantasy chick, I'll do something worse than make you watch Bill give me oral pleasure.

PISTON: Oh, God!

BILL: What a wimp.

(BILL *and* BELLA *turn to go.*)

PISTON: Not so fast, Bella. I know you and Bill murdered Hermosa, and I won't rest until you pay! Although, maybe I should wait until you untie me to make such threats.

BELLA: We already untied you, Piston. About twenty minutes ago.

BILL: You must be cramping up.

BELLA: I know what you know, Piston, and you
don't know nothing. Everything Cabal had us do—
the cleanups, the coverups, the cattle mutilations—

BILL: Bella...

BELLA: Oh, you don't know about that. Never mind.
—Everything she done, she done to preserve the
reputation of the hotel.

PISTON: Does that include burning it to the ground?

BELLA: She was a wacko.

BILL: Wack. O.

BELLA: She wanted that employee-of-the-month award,
and she wasn't gonna let nothing stand in her way.
But she never would have harmed a paying customer.
And that's what Herberto Hermosa was. A paying
customer. And me and Bill, you're right, we got our
hands in a lot of pies.

(BILL *shows his hand, it's covered with pie.*)

BELLA: But just because you uncovered a conspiracy,
don't mean it's the same conspiracy that hired them
aliens to kidnap your sister, Agent Mulder.

BILL: Bella...

BELLA: Damn. I keep forgetting how far out of the loop
you are. Where was I?

BILL: Pie.

BELLA: So you can come after us if you want, Piston.
But it won't get you any closer to your fantasy chick.
And the real werewolf is slipping away.

BILL: Or getting closer.

BELLA: Or maybe staying in one place.

BILL: Or moving kinda back and forth like this...

(BILL *moves back and forth.*)

BELLA: Actually, who knows what he's doing?

BILL: Not us.

PISTON: Yeah, I got that. And why should I believe you?

(BELLA *pulls out a whip.*)

PISTON: Oh, God. Oh God. Oh God.

(*She dangles it in front of his nose.*)

PISTON: Ew! Ew! Yuck! Ew! All right, I believe you!

(BELLA *puts the whip away.*)

BELLA: We like you, Piston

BILL: You're funny.

BELLA: Don't make us kill you.

BILL: And your family.

(BILL *and* BELLA *exit.*)

PISTON: (*To the audience:*) Why did I believe Bill and
Bella? Two of the most dangerous hired serial killers
In the Northern Hemisphere? Well...oh God...without
getting too much into...oh God...emotional recall, let me
just say that I've heard them howl...and I've seen them...
ugh... Let's just say they're not convincing canines, okay?
Can we just change the subject? Oh God, I'm gonna be
sick again.
(*He runs out.*)

LARRY'S STUDIO

(LARRY *glares at* TODD *who backs slowly away from the the
piano.*)

SPIKE: Larry! You're alive! Again! Oh, Larry, I'm so glad
to see you. Oh, Larry. I missed you so much. When you

were lying there dead, all I could think about was so
many things. You know all the stuff you never get to
say to somebody until it's too late, and then it's too late.

(LARRY *still stares at* TODD *who is paralyzed with fear.*)

SPIKE: It all happened so quick. One minute you were
there, and the next minute you were... (*She points kinda
down at the ground:*) ...there. I just couldn't believe you
were gone. And I guess you weren't gone, so I guess
I was right not to believe, wasn't I, Larry? Oh, Larry,
I'll never believe you again. I don't mean that the way
it came out. I mean the next time you're dead, I won't—
Well, not that you were dead last time. Obviously.
Were you? I mean, I saw you shot down in cold blood,
Larry. Twice! Didn't I? How could you have survived
that? Unless you didn't survive? Or unless... Oh, no.
Larry, you're not...you're not...Larry, are you...?

(LARRY *turns to* SPIKE.)

SPIKE: I'm sorry, Larry. I've got so many questions
running round in my head right now. Who was that
guy? Why did he shoot you? Why did the other guy
shoot you? Who was he? What about the record
contract? What about Todd? Why doesn't someone
shoot Todd? I hate Todd. Why are you looking at me
like that? Who are you? What are you? Why are you
here? Do you eat red meat? Do I count as red meat?
But I know you don't like to talk about these kinda
things sometimes, so I'm only gonna ask you one thing.
One thing, Larry. (*Pause*) Can we get married now?

BLACKOUT

EPISODE 14

"Mrs Hermosa is a colleague of mine. My interest in her
is strictly collegiate."

CHARACTERS

HARLEQUIN
FANTASY DICK
FANTASY CHICK
WOLFGANG BIEDERMANN
HERBERTO HERMOSA
ALFREDO CENTAURI
MARCUS BENIGNUS
DICK PISTON
LARRY FINGERS
SPIKE
TODD MORTON
BELLA BOLA

HARLEQUIN

HARLEQUIN: LARRY AND THE WEREWOLF. Episode Fourteen! Awooooo...

FANTASY

(FANTASY CHICK *pulls open the front of her wetsuit, revealing a Delta Delta Delta sorority sweater.*)

FANTASY CHICK: I'm your little sister.

FANTASY DICK: You're a Tri-Delt.

FANTASY CHICK: And you're Sigma Chi.

FANTASY DICK: I remember you now.

FANTASY CHICK: I used to follow you around.

FANTASY DICK: They called you the girl who couldn't say "no"

FANTASY CHICK: The boys couldn't say "no" either. *(Pause)* Except for you.

FANTASY DICK: I had other interests.

FANTASY CHICK: Detective work?

FANTASY DICK: I was in love.

FANTASY CHICK: And you let that stand in the way of cheap, easy sex?

FANTASY DICK: I knew you wouldn't understand.

FANTASY CHICK: What was her name?

FANTASY DICK: I never asked.

FANTASY CHICK: Was she a Tri-Delt?

FANTASY DICK: She was you.

(FANTASY CHICK *takes him in her arms and kisses him. They gaze into each others' eyes and he says...*)

FANTASY DICK: Come on, we've got work to do.

ALFREDO'S APARTMENT

(ALFREDO *is contemplating a cigar, as* BIEDERMANN *and* HERMOSA *look on.*)

BIEDERMANN: Okay, this is boring. What do you say, next redhead who comes in, we haunt her.

HERMOSA: What if it's a man?

BIEDERMANN: A what?

HERMOSA: What if the redhead is a man. We still haunt him, right?

BIEDERMANN: I dunno. Red headed guys make me think of Opie.

HERMOSA: Chauvinist.

BIEDERMANN: Tell you what, next person comes in wearing a skirt, male or female, *that's* who we haunt.

(MARCUS BENIGNUS *comes in wearing a gladiator costume with a skirted cuirass.*)

BIEDERMANN: Does not count! Does not count!

(MARCUS BENIGNUS *hands* ALFREDO *a martini and goes out.* PISTON *bursts in, gun in hand.*)

PISTON: Centauri!

ALFREDO: Piston.

BIEDERMANN & HERMOSA: PISTON*!!*

PISTON: Oh no.

BIEDERMANN & HERMOSA: Woo!

ALFREDO: You are just the man I am looking for.

BIEDERMANN: We missed you, Piston.

HERMOSA: How'd you get out of the coma?

BIEDERMANN: Hey, guess what we found out!

HERMOSA: Guess who killed me!

PISTON: Shut up.

(PISTON *fires his gun into the air, shutting the ghosts up.*)

BIEDERMANN: *(Covering his ears:)* Ow.

PISTON: *(To* ALFREDO:*)* You, sit down. *(To ghosts:)*
You and you, over there where I can see you.

HERMOSA: But, Piston—

PISTON: Shut up!!

BIEDERMANN: You're gonna be sorry you talked to us
like that.

ALFREDO: Are you all right, Mister Piston? You seem
distracted.

PISTON: You don't seem very surprised to see me.

ALFREDO: Should I be? You are a resourceful man. It
was only a matter of time before you tracked me down.

PISTON: You have a lot of confidence in my
investigative abilities, considering I was dead.

ALFREDO: Were you? I'm sorry I missed that.

PISTON: Trapped in a burning building. Fell ten stories.
And murdered in the hospital. Sound familiar?

ALFREDO: Not yet. How does it end?

PISTON: You mean to tell me that you didn't know I was dead? Twice.

ALFREDO: No, you seem to have inferred it. Brilliant.

PISTON: It was in all the papers.

ALFREDO: I don't read the papers. So full of lies mostly. It was papers who said Herberto Hermosa committed suicide.

PISTON: Yes, but we both know he was murdered.

ALFREDO: Yes.

PISTON: By a werewolf.

ALFREDO: Yes.

PISTON: You're a werewolf.

(Pause)

ALFREDO: Perhaps you are wondering why I called you here, Mister Piston.

PISTON: I came of my own volition.

ALFREDO: Did you?

(ALFREDO *laughs. The ghosts laugh, too.)*

BIEDERMANN: He zenned for you.

BIEDERMANN & HERMOSA: Pissstonnn... Pissstonnn...

ALFREDO: I have a proposal for you. *(He throws down a stack of twenty dollar bills.)*

PISTON: You can't bribe me.

(ALFREDO *opens a briefcase full of similar bundles.)*

PISTON: You can bribe me.

(PISTON *reaches for the money, but* ALFREDO *snaps the briefcase shut.)*

ALFREDO: I don't want to bribe you. I want to hire you.

PISTON: I've already got a case.

ALFREDO: Perhaps it's the same case. This one involves Larry Fingers.

BIEDERMANN & HERMOSA: Take the case! Take the case!

PISTON: Ssh!!

ALFREDO: *(Whispers:)* This one involves Larry Fingers. Helga Hermosa is in love with him. But he is wrong for her.

PISTON: And who's right for her, Alfredo? You?

ALFREDO: Larry Fingers is evil.

PISTON: That's your story.

HERMOSA: No, he's right, Piston.

PISTON: Shut up.

BIEDERMANN: Piston—

PISTON: Shut up! *(To* ALFREDO:*)* This is the second time you've tried to pin the murder on Larry Fingers, but let me tell you the story the way I see it. A handsome Italian man named Alfredo comes to America where he meets and falls in love with a beautiful young woman named Helga.

ALFREDO: Roman.

PISTON: Hmm?

ALFREDO: I think the man in your story is Roman. Not Italian.

PISTON: *(Irritably:)* Rome is *in* Italy.

*(*ALFREDO *takes a moment to remember whether that is correct.)*

ALFREDO: So it is.

PISTON: But Helga doesn't love Alfredo. Instead she falls for a dashing hispanic fellow named Herberto.

HERMOSA: Nah. She married me for my money.

BIEDERMANN: And you're kinda clumsy.

HERMOSA: Why you—

(HERMOSA *and* BIEDERMANN *scuffle.*)

PISTON: Unfortunately for Helga, Alfredo is the jealous type. Unfortunately for Herberto, Alfredo is also the werewolf type. So when Helga spurns Alfredo to marry her true love Herberto...

(*Glancing at* HERMOSA *who is wrestling around on the floor with* BIEDERMANN:)

PISTON: ...for his money... Alfredo follows them to the hotel on their honeymoon night, turns into that werewolf and murders the groom.

ALFREDO: Waitaminute, you lost me. The handsome Italian murders Mister Hermosa out of love for Mister Hermosa's wife?

PISTON: Yes.

ALFREDO: If he loves her, why would he do such a thing? Will she not hate him forever?

PISTON: Love makes men do crazy things.

(MARCUS BENIGNUS *enters in sequined bondage gear with another martini.*)

MARCUS BENIGNUS: Oops.

(MARCUS BENIGNUS *turns quickly and goes back out.*)

ALFREDO: It's all right, Marcus, come in here.

(MARCUS BENIGNUS *comes back in.*)

ALFREDO: Mister Piston has just told me a very amusing story. (*He chuckles amusedly.*) He seems to think I am in love with Helga Hermosa.

(ALFREDO *laughs.* MARCUS BENIGNUS *does not.*)

ALFREDO: You see, Mister Piston, I am what you would call a homosexual.

BIEDERMANN: *(Finally putting two and two together:)* That's what they were doing!

HERMOSA: I could have told you that.

BIEDERMANN: I thought he was helping him pack.

ALFREDO: Mrs Hermosa is a colleague of mine. My interest in her is strictly collegiate.

MARCUS BENIGNUS: *(To ALFREDO:)* Platonic.

ALFREDO: Platonic.

PISTON: You work at the hospital?

ALFREDO: *(To MARCUS BENIGNUS:)* That explains the white uniform.

MARCUS BENIGNUS: *(To ALFREDO:)* And the years in med school.

ALFREDO: *(To PISTON:)* Yes, I am what you would call a doctor. Nurse Helga and I had a falling out over her choice of husband.

PISTON: So you killed him.

ALFREDO: So I was not invited to the wedding. You have quite an imagination.

PISTON: I should write a book.

ALFREDO: I am somewhat old-fashioned, Mister Piston. I could not condone a woman marrying a man simply for his bunny.

PISTON: Bunny?

MARCUS BENIGNUS *(To ALFREDO:)* I think he said "money".

ALFREDO: Money? Yes, of course, *that's* what I objected to.

PISTON: Then why did you say, "bunny"?

ALFREDO: My aneurism must be acting up. Marcus, fetch me my medication.

(MARCUS BENIGNUS *pours another martini.*)

ALFREDO: I tried to tell her things would turn out badly. And they did. Helga is not lucky in love.

HERMOSA: I know the feeling.

ALFREDO: Now, I'm afraid she is in love again. With Larry Fingers. But Larry Fingers will destroy her, Mister Piston. He is a monster. I have tried to warn her. She will not listen to me. But you... (*He opens the briefcase full of money.*) I am hiring you, Dick Piston, to talk to her. Convince her. Stop her before she marries again. If you can put an end to this affair with Larry Fingers. I will pay you one million dollars.

(PISTON *reaches for the money, but* ALFREDO *snaps the briefcase shut again.*)

ALFREDO: Will you do it?

BIEDERMANN & HERMOSA: Yes! Yes! Say, yes!

PISTON: No.

BIEDERMANN & HERMOSA: What? Piston, take the case! Take the case!

PISTON: This doesn't change the fact that somebody killed Hermosa.

BIEDERMANN & HERMOSA: Fingers! It's Fingers!

PISTON: And I think it's you.

BIEDERMANN & HERMOSA: No, Fingers! It's Larry Fingers!

PISTON: You're a werewolf.

BIEDERMANN & HERMOSA: Fingers is the murderer!
We saw him! He's the one.

PISTON: And you murdered Herberto Hermosa
because—

BIEDERMANN & HERMOSA: Fingers! Get Fingers!
He did it!

PISTON: Because he—

BIEDERMANN & HERMOSA: Fingerrrrrrrs! Fingerrrrrrrs!
Fingerrrrrrrs!

PISTON: I'm going to look into this Fingers thing.
But I'll be back.

LARRY'S STUDIO

(LARRY *is addressing wedding invitations.* SPIKE *comes in
with several more.*)

SPIKE: Which pile is outgoing?

(LARRY *points to a pile of envelopes.* SPIKE *adds her
envelopes to the stack and flips through the ones* LARRY *has
aleady addressed.*)

SPIKE: Moammar and Mrs Kadhafi? Saddam Hussein
and Guest? Larry, why are you inviting these people
to the wedding? They're not gonna come. John Gotti?
Frank Sinatra? Sammy "The Bull" Doe? Some of these
people I've never even heard of. Helga Hermosa?
Who is that?

(LARRY *shrugs.*)

SPIKE: Do you know any of these people?

(LARRY *is silent.* SPIKE *throws* LARRY's *invitations in the
trash. She throws the* HELGA *letter in last.*)

SPIKE: Larry, it's okay to have an intimate ceremony. We don't have to send out five hundred invitations just 'cause that's how many came in the box.

(LARRY *nods.* SPIKE *gives him a hug.*)

SPIKE: Have you seen Todd?

(LARRY *shakes his head.*)

SPIKE: Todd!! (*She goes out.*)

(LARRY *reaches into the trash and takes out one envelope and puts it back in the stack.*)

TODD MORTON'S FAVORITE BAR

(BELLA *is dressed like a Vegas showgirl.* TODD *swaggers up to her.*)

TODD: What's a nice girl like you doing in a place like this?

BELLA: Lookin' for a nice guy like you to get me drunk and fuck my brains out. Buy you a beer?

TODD: (*Shaken:*) Uh...I guess, yeah.

(BELLA *goes off to get a beer.*)

TODD: (*Shouting off to her:*) You know this doesn't happen every day! (*Pause*) You know, I think I'm in love with you! (*Pause*) And not just because you're dressed like I always fantasized my future wife would be when I finally met her! ...Or at least on our honeymoon!

(BELLA *returns with two mugs of beer.*)

BELLA: That's a charming story.

(BELLA *turns her back to* TODD *and puts something in his drink.*)

TODD: Hey! Did you just put something in my drink?

BELLA: Nope.

TODD: Yes, you did, I just saw you!

BELLA: Ssh...

(BELLA *leans toward* TODD *and kisses away his objections.*)

TODD: *(Dreamily:)* There's only one thing that could make this moment perfect.

BELLA: I'm wet.

(TODD *faints dead away.* BELLA *pours her beer on him.* TODD *recovers.*)

TODD: What's your name?

BELLA: Bella.

TODD: My name's Todd.

BELLA: Hi, Todd.

TODD: Todd Morton. It means death in two languages.

(BELLA *turns her back to* TODD *and takes something out of his beer.*)

BELLA: Well, now it means death in three.

TODD: You just slipped something into my drink again!

BELLA: No, I didn't.

TODD: I *saw* you!

BELLA: Gee, I'd better go get another beer. *(She exits.)*

(TODD *looks in his drink. He puts his hand in the mug, and feels around until he pulls something out. It's a hand grenade.* TODD *opens his mouth to scream.*)

BLACKOUT

EPISODE 15

"There's no point wearing a fitted suit if you're not gonna wear the right holster with it."

CHARACTERS

HARLEQUIN
SPIKE
LARRY FINGERS
BILL BOLA
BELLA BOLA
HELGA HERMOSA
WOLFGANG BIEDERMANN
HERBERTO HERMOSA
DICK PISTON
THE SPANISH GHOST

HARLEQUIN

(HARLEQUIN *picks up a discarded wedding invitation, and opens it.*)

HARLEQUIN: "The parents of Scheherezade "Spike" Snodgrass—deceased—request the honor of your presence at the marriage of their daughter Spike Elizabeth to Mister Larry Fingers, reception immediately following." *(Pockets the invitation)* I'd be delighted!

LARRY AND THE WEREWOLF. Episode Fifteen! Awooooo...

LOBBY OF THE CHURCH

(LARRY *in a tux, pacing.* LARRY *clears his throat.*)

SPIKE: *(Offstage:)* Larry! Close your eyes!

(SPIKE *enters in a wedding dress with her hands over her eyes.* LARRY *looks at her.*)

SPIKE: It's bad luck for the bride and groom to see each other before the wedding, but this is an emergency. Have you seen Todd? It's almost time, and he's not here yet. Ordinarily, I'd say good riddance, but he *is* your best man—God knows why—and he's got the rings, Larry. We can't start without him.

(LARRY *reaches into his pocket and pulls out the rings. Gives one to* SPIKE.)

SPIKE: Oh. Well, that's okay then. Never mind. I'm sorry I panicked, Larry.

(LARRY *exits.*)

SPIKE: Do you like my dress? No, wait, don't look. Never mind. It's white. I think that's okay, don't you? I mean, I'm still basically a virgin, except for those guys when I was a prostitute. I guess I shouldn't say that so loud, this is a church after all. Y'know, Larry... this has all happened so fast, we haven't really had a chance to talk about it and... Well, I would like to say that marrying you makes me the happiest girl in the world. I'd like to, but I can't, because... just being onstage with you night after night already makes me the happiest girl in the world. So this is gravy. Er... no, that probably doesn't sound as romantic as I meant it to be. What I guess I'm trying to say is... (*Long pause*) I love you, Larry. (*She blushes.*) No, no! Don't speak. I'll see you at the altar. (*She blows a kiss. And exits.*)

OUTSIDE THE CHAPEL

(BELLA *and* BILL *enter, dressed for a wedding.*)

BELLA: (*Straightening his lapels for him:*) Look at you. You're bulging all over the place. There's no point wearing a fitted suit if you're not gonna wear the right holster with it.

(*Enter* HARLEQUIN *from the chapel, as the usher.*)

HARLEQUIN: Friends of the bride or friends of the groom?

BELLA: We'd rather not say.

(HARLEQUIN *escorts them into the chapel.* HELGA *enters, dressed in mourning.* HARLEQUIN *returns.*)

HARLEQUIN: Bride or groom?

HELGA: Groom. (*She shows* HARLEQUIN *her invitation. Whispers:*) I'm his lover!

(HARLEQUIN *escorts her into the chapel.* BIEDERMANN *and* HERMOSA *enter.*)

HERMOSA: Where's Piston?

BIEDERMANN: He went to park the car.

HERMOSA: He'd better hurry, or he's gonna miss the ceremony.

BIEDERMANN: He'll make it, don't worry, we better get our seats.

HARLEQUIN: Friends of the bride or groom?

HERMOSA: Boy, that's a tough one.

BIEDERMANN: Yeah, we don't know the bride.

HERMOSA: But then the groom is the one who killed me. So I don't think you'd call us friends, exactly.

BIEDERMANN: So bride. We'll say bride.

(HARLEQUIN *escorts them into the chapel.*)

DICK PISTON

PISTON: (*To the audience:*) The wedding of Larry Fingers and Spike. The proverbial frosting on the cake of corruption and deceipt that had taken me to hell and back. The case of Larry and the Werewolf was about to break wide open.

(*The music of the processional is heard.* PISTON *looks at his watch.*)

PISTON: And I have just enough time to reload. (*He takes out his gun.*)

THE CHAPEL

(The traditional wedding processional becomes a funky jazz number with LARRY *on keyboards. Lights strobe and lasers flash as* SPIKE *is flown in on wires, dressed in a sumptuous bridal gown. She grabs a microphone and announces...)*

SPIKE: Ladieeeeeeeees and Gentlemennnnnnnn! The musical marriage of Larryyyyyyyyyy Fingerrrrrrrrs! Aaaaaaand Spike! *(To herself:)* Where's that fucking Todd? I can't believe I have to introduce myself at my own wedding. *(To the priest:)* Hit it, preacher.

*(*HARLEQUIN *enters as the priest.* SPIKE *tosses him the microphone.)*

HARLEQUIN: *(Intones:)* Dearly beloved, we are gathered here today in the sight of these present to join this man

HERMOSA: Booo!

HARLEQUIN: And this woman in bonds of holy matrimony. If there is anyone here who can show just cause why they should not be wed Let them speak now, or forever hold their peace.

(Music ceases and lights return to normal, as everyone looks out over the audience. Pause. No one objects, so the wedding is about to proceed, when...)

HELGA: *(Appalled:)* What, am I the only one???

SPIKE: What the hell is she doing here?

(She looks at LARRY. LARRY *shrugs.)*

HELGA: *(To the wedding guests:)* I can't believe this. You people should all be ashamed of yourselves. Shame on you. Shame! Shame! Shame! Well, I guess I can see where this is headed. All right, go on, go ahead with this travesty, don't let me stop you. I know when I'm outvoted.

(HELGA *sits and pouts.* LARRY *plays the accompaniment as* HARLEQUIN *continues.*)

HARLEQUIN: Do you Scheherezade Snodgrass—not her real name—take this man, Larry Fingers

HERMOSA: Booo!

HARLEQUIN: To be your lawful wedded husb—

SPIKE: *(Quickly:)* I do.

HARLEQUIN: —to have and to hold—

SPIKE: Yes, I do.

HARLEQUIN: —Love, honor and cherish.

SPIKE: Yes.

HARLEQUIN: Now and forever.

SPIKE: Yes.

HARLEQUIN: For richer—

SPIKE: Yes.

HARLEQUIN: For poorer—

SPIKE: Yes.

HARLEQUIN: In sickness

SPIKE: Yes.

HARLEQUIN: And in health

SPIKE: Yes.

HARLEQUIN: Till death do you part?

SPIKE: Yes, yes, I do, I do! *(She snatches the microphone away from* HARLEQUIN *and sings.)*
For richer for poorer
To have and to hold.

I'll honor love and cherish him
Until we're grey and old.

In sick and in healthy
From now till we're dead.
I'll take him and I'll make him
be my husband lawful wed!

I love you Larry!
I do, I do!
I love you Larry, cuz I've very, Larry, much in love
with you.
I do, I do!!

(HELGA *weeps uncontrollably.*)

HARLEQUIN: And do you, Larry Fingers...

HERMOSA: Booo!

HARLEQUIN: Take this woman, Spike, to be your lawful
wedded wife. To have and to hold. To love, honor
and cherish. Now and forever. For richer, for poorer.
In sickness and in health. Till death do you part?

(HARLEQUIN *hands* LARRY *the microphone. Pause*)

SPIKE: Larry?

(Pause)

HELGA: Stop! I can't let this go on. *(She leaps up to the
altar.)*

SPIKE: What are you doing?

HELGA: I could ask you the same question.

SPIKE: I'm getting married.

HELGA: Oh, Larry, you're making a terrible mistake.
Just look at her! Ugh. Now look at me. Oo! Her, ugh.
Me, oo. Her, ugh. Me, oo.

SPIKE: Larry, why is she talking to you like this?

HELGA: *(To* SPIKE:*)* Excuse me, could we have some privacy?!

SPIKE: This is our wedding!

HELGA: *(To* LARRY:*)* You're doing this to punish me, aren't you? And I was bad. I was very bad. I only married Herberto to make you jealous. And because he was rich.

BIEDERMANN: *(To* HERMOSA:*)* Aren't you going to stand up for yourself?

HERMOSA: *(Stands up:)* Hey!

HELGA: And because he had a cute butt.

HERMOSA: Yes!

(HERMOSA *high fives* BIEDERMANN, *then he jumps up on the dais and moons* LARRY.)

HERMOSA: Read it and weep, Fingers!

BIEDERMANN: Oh, now that's tacky, put your pants on.

HELGA: I know you're only marrying your roadie to get back at me.

SPIKE: Hey! I'm in the band!

HELGA: But you still love me, Larry, I know you do. I can see it in your eyes.

SPIKE: Gimme those eyes! *(To* LARRY:*)* Say it ain't so, Larry.

(PISTON *bursts into the chapel with his gun drawn.)*

PISTON: *(To* LARRY:*)* Put your hands where I can see them and step away from the bride. *(To* SPIKE:*)* Larry, ain't gonna say it ain't so, cuz it is so, Spike. Larry and Helga were an item. Until she left him for Herberto Hermosa.

HERMOSA: Because I have a cute butt.

PISTON: So Larry killed him.

HELGA: But you said Herberto was killed by a werewolf.

PISTON: Larry is a werewolf. Beneath that calm cool exterior, lurks an angry furry exterior.

SPIKE: Those are serious accusations, Piston, and they're ridiculous! Where's your proof?

PISTON: I don't have any.

HERMOSA: Whatta ya mean? Look at me! I'm living proof.

BIEDERMANN: But you're dead.

HERMOSA: Well, then who should know better? (*Ghostly:*) I am the ghost of Herberto Hermosa, and Larry Fingers murdered me in cold blood. And he was a werewolf at the time.

(*Beat*)

PISTON: I can't tell you how I know, but I know. Larry and the Werewolf are the same man. ...Wolf.

HERMOSA: Nobody's gonna believe you, just shoot him.

SPIKE: Is this true, Larry? Raise your right hand, and swear to me that you're not a beastly demonic hellspawn. And remember, you're in a house of God.

(LARRY *takes a step toward* PISTON.)

PISTON: I wouldn't try it, Larry. These might be silver bullets.

(BILL *and* BELLA *draw their weapons.*)

BELLA: All right, put the gun down, Piston.

PISTON: Bella? What are you doing here?

BELLA: I'd rather not say. But if you don't put the gun down. I'm gonna have to get nasty.

PISTON: I can't, Bella, Larry is the werewolf. Larry is the killer. This is what I came back from the grave to do!

(LARRY *takes another step toward* PISTON. SPIKE *and* HELGA *both try to hold him back.*)

SPIKE: Don't do it, Larry, he'll kill you.

HELGA: Larry, I don't want to lose you.

HERMOSA: *(Taunting* LARRY:*)* I'm gonna haunt you, sucka!

BELLA: All right, Piston, you asked for it.

(BELLA *kisses* BILL.)

PISTON: Oh, God, no!

BELLA: Oh, Bill.

PISTON: Stop it!

SPIKE: *(To* HELGA:*)* He's not yours to lose, he's mine.

HELGA: He was mine, first. Hey! My jewelry!

(HELGA *grabs* SPIKE's *crucifix.*)

SPIKE: Hey, let go. That's mine!

HELGA: That was given to me!

(SPIKE *and* HELGA *fight.* LARRY *begins advancing toward* PISTON)

HERMOSA: *(Haunting* LARRY:*)* Woo!

BELLA: Oh, Bill!

BILL: Oh, Bella!

PISTON: NO!! *(His gun goes off.)*

SPIKE & HELGA: *(Stop fighting:)* NO!!

BELLA: *(Stops kissing:)* NO!!

BILL: *(Doesn't stop:)* YES!!

(LARRY *falls dead.*)

BILL, BELLA, SPIKE & HELGA: NOOO!!!

(Suddenly, in a cloud of smoke and flame, a dashing SPANISH GHOST *appears upon the altar.)*

SPANISH GHOST: I am the ghost of Herberto Hermosa!

BIEDERMANN: Uh oh.

BLACKOUT

FOR THE
LOVE OF
HELGA

EPISODE 16

"Waitaminute. Who all sees ghosts?"

CHARACTERS

HARLEQUIN
THE SPANISH GHOST
WOLFGANG BIEDERMANN
HERBERTO HERMOSA
BILL BOLA
BELLA BOLA
DICK PISTON
HELGA HERMOSA
SPIKE
ALFREDO CENTAURI
LARRY FINGERS

HARLEQUIN

*(The others remain frozen in their wedding tableau,
as* HARLEQUIN *appears...)*

HARLEQUIN: Awooooo... *(Pause, he surveys the scene,
waiting for just the right moment...)* ...LARRY AND
THE WEREWOLF. Episode Sixteen!

THE CHAPEL

SPANISH GHOST: I am the ghost of Herberto Hermosa!

BIEDERMANN: *(To* HERMOSA:*)* I thought *you* were the
ghost of Herberto Hermosa.

HERMOSA: I am, I'm the ghost of Herberto Hermosa.
(Ghostly:) I am the ghost of Herberto Hermosa!

BIEDERMANN: Where's your accent?

HERMOSA: I am not going to dignify that racist remark.

BIEDERMANN: *This* guy has an accent.

HERMOSA: You're just a big bigot, *Wolfgang. Sieg Heil!
Sieg Heil! Sieg Heil!*

BIEDERMANN: Rrr. Somebody hold me back.

*(*HERMOSA *ducks behind* PISTON.*)*

HERMOSA: You gotta believe me, Piston. I'm the ghost
of Herberto Hermosa. Larry killed me. I saw it with my
own eyes. Quick, shoot him some more.

BELLA: Larry didn't kill you. I did.

HERMOSA: Bella!! ...I mean... That's a lie!!

PISTON: What?? Waitaminute. Who all sees ghosts?

(BELLA, HELGA, PISTON, BILL *and* BIEDERMANN *all raise their hands.* BELLA *elbows* BILL *and he puts his back down.*)

PISTON: Who all *are* ghosts?

(HERMOSA, BIEDERMANN, *the* SPANISH GHOST *and* BILL *raise their hands.* BELLA *elbows* BILL *and he puts it back down.*)

PISTON: Werewolves?

(BILL *raises his hand.* BELLA *elbows him and he puts it back down.*)

BELLA: He just likes to vote.

SANISH GHOST: Helga!

HELGA: Herberto!

(HELGA *runs to him.*)

PISTON: (*To* HERMOSA:) Then who are you?

BIEDERMANN: Yeah!

HERMOSA: I'm tellin' you, I'm the ghost of Herberto Hermosa. You did the right thing killing Larry Fingers, Piston. In cold blood. In a church.

BELLA: His name is Nikolai Nikolnikov. K G B.

HERMOSA: I've never seen this woman before in my life.

BIEDERMANN: What about after that?

BELLA: I met him when Bill and I were with Israeli Intelligence.

HERMOSA: It was love at first sight.

BELLA: You meant nothing to me.

HERMOSA: (*Sighs:*) Just like the girl who married dear old dad.

BELLA: We were working on a joint-operation to infiltrate Larry's band of international—

(BELLA *catches herself. She and* HERMOSA *exchange frantic glances.*)

BELLA & HERMOSA: Musicians!

BELLA: Yeah.

HERMOSA: Whole band of 'em.

BELLA: Yeah.

(BILL *raises his hand.* BELLA *elbows him and he puts it down.*)

BELLA: The K G B had discovered that Larry has a thing for double-jointed Jewish girls.

HERMOSA: Larry has a thing for a lot of things.

BELLA: So I was brought in to seduce him with my Hassidic wiles. Nikolai, however wanted me all to himself.

HERMOSA: Well, not *all* of you.

BELLA: He was sending me flowers on stakeout. Encrypted love notes. It was embarrassing.

HERMOSA: You were cute in your jackboots.

BELLA: The first time I was with Larry Fingers, Nikolai was on surveillance. And when that first time turned into a second and a third and a fourth...

HERMOSA: I thought they'd never come out of that phone booth.

BELLA: He couldn't take it anymore. He snapped. Bill tried to stop him, but Nikolai burst into the booth and tried to kill Larry. So I killed him first.

HELGA: You killed Larry?

BELLA: No. Nikolai.

HELGA: Who's Nikolai?

BELLA: *(To* HERMOSA*:)* You said he could have me over your dead body.

HERMOSA: That's not what I meant!

HELGA: *(To* SPIKE*:)* Is it me? Am I Nikolai?

BELLA: It was the only way to preserve my cover.

HERMOSA: And I had to float by and watch while the two of them—

PISTON: I get the picture I get the picture I get the picture!

HERMOSA: You blew more than your cover that night, Bella.

BELLA: It was for the mission, Nikolai. You forgot about the mission.

HERMOSA: The only mission you cared about was submission to the erotic machinations of Larry Fingers!

BELLA: *(Remembering:)* Mmmmm... Woof! Whoops. That just slipped out.

SPIKE: Larry, you slept with her?

BELLA: After he died, Nikolai was sent back to haunt me. But he never did.

HERMOSA: I did sometimes.

BELLA: When I'm in the shower.

HERMOSA: Pretend all you want, I see the way you soap up.

BELLA: Instead of avenging himself on the woman who had murdered him, he used his supernatural powers to find a dope he could dupe into killing Larry Fingers. Nice trick, Nick.

HERMOSA: Can I just reiterate that this is all a pack of lies?

PISTON: Yes, it is.

HERMOSA: It is?

PISTON: Call me a nitpicker, if you—

BILL: Nitpicker!

(PISTON *glares at* BILL.)

PISTON: ...if you like, but—

BELLA: Nitpicker!

BILL: Nitpicker!

PISTON: But there's one piece of your—

HELGA: Nitpicker!

PISTON: All right, stop it!! (*He glares at all of them.*) There's one piece of your proverbial puzzle that just doesn't fit, Bella.

HERMOSA: (*Sneers at* BELLA:) Band of musicians...

PISTON: The two of you don't *look* like Israeli spies. And by "the two of you" I mean... Bill.

(BILL *blushes and covers his crotch.*)

BELLA: We had to go into hiding, Piston. The K G B put out a contract on me. So did the Mossad.

BILL: And A T & T.

BELLA: They were the worst.

BILL: Don't mess with Ma.

BELLA: But Larry saved us. He took me to a plastic surgeon. He said it would just be the face. (*She points at her breasts.*) But these came from somewhere!

PISTON: And Bill?

BELLA: Larry bribed a rabbi to do a cosmetic bris.

PISTON: You had him un-circumcised?

BELLA: Completely.

BILL: Wanna see?

BELLA: Bill!

BILL: *(To himself:)* Pants up, hands on gun. Pants up, hands on gun...

BIEDERMANN: *(To* PISTON*:)* You killed the wrong guy again, Piston.

PISTON: So who *did* murder Herberto Hermosa?

(They all turn to look at the SPANISH GHOST.*)*

SPANISH GHOST: I love you, Helga.

HELGA: I know.

SPANISH GHOST: I know you know. But you don't know.

HELGA: I don't?

SPANISH GHOST: No. You don't know that I knew you only married me to make Larry jealous.

HELGA: And for your money.

BIEDERMANN: And his butt.

SPANISH GHOST: You don't know that I knew the danger I was in. I knew that nobody crosses Fingers with impunity.

*(*HELGA *slaps him.)*

SPANISH GHOST: It means "without punishment".

HELGA: Oh. *(Giggles)* You know what I thought it meant...?

SPANISH GHOST: Helga!

HELGA: Herberto!

SPANISH GHOST: I knew it could mean my death, but I had to make you my wife because I saw in you the same helpless innocent that I was before Larry sucked me into his web of lies.

HELGA: *(Sobbing:)* No, no, it's not a web.

SPANISH GHOST: It was Larry who arranged our first meeting.

HELGA: Larry?

SPANISH GHOST: Yes.

HELGA: Nooo!

SPANISH GHOST: It was no coincidence that I was in the hospital that day with a superficial leg wound and a pitcher of margaritas.

HELGA: And that matador outfit. Mrow!

SPANISH GHOST: It was self-inflicted.

HELGA: And the leg wound? Was that self-inflicted, too?

SPANISH GHOST: It was the only way to get close to you. Close enough... To kill you.

HELGA: To kill me?

SPANISH GHOST: Yes.

HELGA: Nooo!

SPANISH GHOST: Larry hired me to kill you.

HELGA: To kill me?

SPANISH GHOST: Yes.

HELGA: Nooo!

SPANISH GHOST: But I couldn't bring myself to do it.

HELGA: To kill me?

SPANISH GHOST: Yes.

HELGA: Nooo!

SPANISH GHOST: You're not really listening, are you?

HELGA: I must be in denial.

SPANISH GHOST: Ya think?

HELGA: Nooo!

PISTON: Excuse me, Mister Hermosa—

SPANISH GHOST: I am not here for you, detective.

BIEDERMANN: Let me try. Hey, buddy—

(*The* SPANISH GHOST *punches* BIEDERMANN *in the nose.*)

SPANISH GHOST: Helga!

HELGA: Herberto!

SPANISH GHOST: I sacrificed myself so that you would know what real self-sacrifice was. So you could see the difference between true love... and Larry Fingers.

HELGA: Yes! It's like difference between apples...and oranges. They're both tasty and you eat 'em with your hands, but they're not the same! They're not the same at all! An orange would never say it loved you and then treat you like a cheap tart, but an apple would! An apple would! Oh, why, Herberto, why did it have to be like this? You seemed like such a promising young...uh...hitman, I guess.

SPANISH GHOST: Because when I looked in your eyes I saw something I'd never seen before.

HELGA: Bunnies?

SPANISH GHOST: I've seen bunnies, Helga.

HELGA: A unicorn?

SPANISH GHOST: I saw a frightened young girl.

HELGA: What was she doing in my eyes?

SPANISH GHOST: A frightened young girl...who needed me.

HELGA: What was she doing in my eyes???!!!

SPANISH GHOST: Helga!

HELGA: Herberto!

SPANISH GHOST: When I met you I realized my entire life's work—all the senseless killings—would be meaningless if I couldn't save you. If I couldn't save you from yourself. And from this monster.

HELGA: He *is* a monster.

PISTON: He's a werewolf.

SPANISH GHOST: He is worse than a werewolf. He is a man. An evil man. With a soul as dark and atonal as the music he plays. A man who does not love. Cannot love. Will not love. Should not love. Forget him, Helga. Leave him. Flee from him, like the monster he is.

HELGA: I will! I will! Oh, Herberto, can you ever forgive me?

SPANISH GHOST: I have forgiven you, already.

(He kisses her.)

HELGA: Herberto, I love you.

SPANISH GHOST: I know.

(The SPANISH GHOST *vanishes in a cloud of sensuous smoke.)*

PISTON: Wait!

HELGA: Larry Fingers...

(She kicks LARRY. *She spits on him. Then she runs out. Then she comes back. She kicks him again. Then she runs out.)*

PISTON: Wait!

(ALFREDO *appears from behind a pillar and hands* PISTON *a briefcase full of money.*)

ALFREDO: Good work, Piston.

SPIKE: *(To* PISTON:*)* You...killed...Larry...for...*money*!!

PISTON: Wait—

(SPIKE *floors* PISTON *with one punch. Then she pounces on him and begins strangling him with her bridal veil.*)

ALFREDO: The money is not for killing Larry Fingers. It is for some legal work Piston did.

SPIKE: Legal work?

(SPIKE *stops strangling* PISTON *who is unconscious by now.*)

ALFREDO: Alienating the affections of Helga Hermosa. Convincing her to desert this lecherous, libidinous ravager, this vile seducer, this pathological destroyer of young women's hearts. Larry Fingers. He's all yours now.

SPIKE: All mine?? He's dead. Piston shot him!

ALFREDO: But did he shoot him with silver bullets?

SPIKE: Yes.

ALFREDO: That doesn't work.

(LARRY *sits up.*)

SPIKE: Larry! You're alive! ...*Again!!*

BELLA: It's gonna take more than a hotel detective to stop Larry Fingers. A whole lot more.

BLACKOUT

EPISODE 17

"My handwriting, my stationery, and this looks like my blood."

CHARACTERS

HARLEQUIN
WOLFGANG BIEDERMANN
HERBERTO HERMOSA
BILL BOLA
BELLA BOLA
LARRY FINGERS
SPIKE
FANTASY DICK
FANTASY CHICK
DICK PISTON
GAIUS LUCIUS
MARCUS BENIGNUS
ALFREDO CENTAURI
HELGA HERMOSA

HARLEQUIN

HARLEQUIN: LARRY AND THE WEREWOLF. Episode Seventeen! Awooooo...

OUTSIDE THE CHURCH

(HELGA *comes out of the church and runs away.* ALFREDO *comes out of the church and runs off after her.* BIEDERMANN *comes out of the church and runs away.* HERMOSA *runs off after him.* BILL *dive-rolls out of the church with* BELLA *who covers him as he springs to his feet and runs away, then she runs off after him.* SPIKE *comes out of the church and runs away. When nobody pursues her, she returns and goes back into the church, slamming the door behind her.*)

INSIDE THE CHAPEL

(PISTON *lies unconscious on the floor.* LARRY *sits next to him, brooding.* LARRY *picks up* PISTON'*s gun, looks in the chamber. He removes one bullet and spins the chamber. Then he points it at* PISTON'*s head...and pulls the trigger. Click.* LARRY *spins the chamber again. Enter* SPIKE.)

SPIKE: Larry?

(LARRY *looks at her. Beat.* LARRY *puts the gun down.*)

SPIKE: I'm kinda mad at you, y'know.

(LARRY *pretends to ignore her.*)

SPIKE: You know, it's not the international espionage or the links to organized crime that bothers me most. And

it's not the other women. It's the lying. No, it's the
women. No, it's the lying. How can we have a life
together if I can't trust you to be honest with me once
in awhile? I mean, I got my share of secrets too. You
know that. Things I would never tell nobody. But I told
you. Stuff you know about me could put me away for
life. Longer if they make me serve consecutively. But
I told you everything, Larry. I got no secrets from you.
Of course I guess I gotta trust you, 'cause of how you
saved me and all, and I guess I ain't never done nothin'
like that for you. But this still ain't no way to treat me,
Larry. I'm your wife. Or gonna be. ...But we all make
mistakes. I guess that's the thing, isn't it? You know
how awful I been. But you never let that stand between
us. You never made me feel like some kinda criminal,
just because of... well, my criminal record and all.
(Pause) Larry, I could forgive you for everything—
the other women, and the betraying your country,
and lying, and all the other women—if you can promise
me one thing... No more other women, okay? Can you
promise me that, Larry?

(LARRY *says nothing.* SPIKE *slumps.*)

SPIKE: ...Larry ...I forgive you. That's the way it should
be, don'tcha think? Love should be unconditional.
...Yeah.

(LARRY *still says nothing.*)

SPIKE: You're awful quiet today. *(She takes out a wedding
ring.)* I know this wasn't how you planned it. And a lot
has happened and... Well, we've still got the rings, and
I know we don't have a priest, but then you never did
believe in God, so... Larry Fingers. I love you. Forever
and ever and ever. No matter what. See this ring?
That's what that means.

(SPIKE *puts the ring on* LARRY's *finger.*)

SPIKE: With this ring, I thee wed.

(LARRY *looks at the ring on his finger for a long moment. Then he removes the ring and hands it back to her. On the verge of tears,* SPIKE *turns to leave, but* LARRY *stops her with a "hand it over" gesture. Trembling,* SPIKE *removes the gold crucifix from her neck, and hands it to* LARRY. *Then she bursts into tears and runs offstage.* LARRY *puts the crucifix around his neck and continues to brood.*)

FANTASY

FANTASY DICK: *(In the darkness:)* It was almost the perfect crime. Not that the crime was so perfect, but the victim was damn close. Most detectives would give their right arm for a client this...cooperative. I had no leads, no suspects, and no cigarettes. But I coulda spent hours probing her for details. A voice told me it wasn't the details I was really after. But I told the voice to shut up and kiss me again.

FANTASY CHICK: *(In the darkness:)* Dick Piston...

FANTASY DICK: *(In the darkness:)* You need me?

FANTASY CHICK: *(In the darkness:)* I need a cigarette.

FANTASY DICK: *(In the darkness:)* Uh oh.

(Lights snap up on FANTASY DICK *coming out of his office.)*

FANTASY DICK: *(To someone inside:)* Wait right there. I'm just gonna run down to the corner.

(Turning to go, he realizes he hasn't left the office. The FANTASY CHICK *is there, too.)*

FANTASY DICK: What the—?

FANTASY CHICK: Dick? I thought you left.

FANTASY DICK: I thought I left, too. This doesn't make any sense.

FANTASY CHICK: I got your note.

FANTASY DICK: I didn't leave you a note.

FANTASY CHICK: Then who's it for?

FANTASY DICK: I didn't leave anyone a note.

FANTASY CHICK: It's your handwriting.

(*She shows him a note.*)

FANTASY DICK: My handwriting, my stationery,
and this looks like my blood.

FANTASY CHICK: What's it say?

FANTASY DICK: "To whom it may concern. You know
who you are. I've got a secret. You've got one, too. You
show me yours. And mine will show you. Sincerely...
Unsigned." This is nonsense. Where did you find it?

FANTASY CHICK: In the ephedra.

FANTASY DICK: The what?

FANTASY CHICK: The philodendron. Fastened from the
fronds.

FANTASY DICK: What??

FANTASY CHICK: Find the philosophaster, find the
phasmid.

FANTASY DICK: You're not making any sense.

FANTASY CHICK: Pheromonal effluvium.

FANTASY DICK: (*Shaking her:*) You're not making any
sense!

THE CHAPEL

PISTON: (*Barely conscious:*) ...not...making...any...sense...

ROME—TWELVE B C

(A Visigoth caravan lies in ruins. A voice can be heard, faintly...)

VOICE: *Effua for fanom. Fen a fenga t'fima. Feh. Sui feh far favla...*

(Enter the three Roman Centurions. They examine the wreckage.)

MARCUS BENIGNUS: Visigoths. They must have been surprised in the night.

ALFREDO: Their bodies are warm. We're getting close.

GAIUS LUCIUS: Why, Centurion? Why are we close? Why are we pursuing him still?

ALFREDO: What are you suggesting, Gaius Lucius? That we let him escape? When he's almost in our grasp?

GAIUS LUCIUS: I'm suggesting that we have more important concerns now than grasping this creature.

ALFREDO: What? What could be more important than stalking the beast that slew us?

GAIUS LUCIUS: Why we're not dead. That's one thing.

MARCUS BENIGNUS: Gaius Lucius is right. We saw what he did to us. We're lucky to be alive. How can we hope to survive another encounter?

GAIUS LUCIUS: Lucky? Your guts were splattered all over the hillside. This is not luck, it's sorcery.

MARCUS BENIGNUS: *(Pointing at the crucifix:)* It's that thing. It's turned us into walking phantoms. Destroy it. That will break the curse.

ALFREDO: Silence. We are not cursed. We are not lucky. I told you, Marcus Benignus, this is not our day to die. The gods are with us. We cannot fail.

GAIUS LUCIUS: You're mad.

ALFREDO: Mad like a fox.

MARCUS BENIGNUS: Like a crazy fox.

ALFREDO: A crazy fox with Roman blood flowing in it's veins, who will never cease till I've had my revenge on that creature.

GAIUS LUCIUS: Why would there be Roman blood in a fox? What an asinine analogy!

MARCUS BENIGNUS: (*Grabbing the crucifix:*) Give me that thing. We've got to burn it.

GAIUS LUCIUS: I've had it with this lunacy, I'm going back to Rome.

ALFREDO: With those scars? What will you tell them? We are demons now, or worse. We are alive for one purpose. To avenge ourselves upon the creature that killed us. And like it or not, you are with me.

GAIUS LUCIUS: We're chasing our tails!

ALFREDO: I am not chasing my tail!

GAIUS LUCIUS: You're chasing somebody's! And it's not mine, 'cause I'm taking my tail and going home.

ALFREDO: I am *not chasing my tail*!!

(ALFREDO *and* GAIUS LUCIUS *growl at each other like animals.*)

MARCUS BENIGNUS: Please, I think if we just burn this thing, we'll all feel a whole lot better.

VOICE: ...*fenua fen feng*...

GAIUS LUCIUS: What's that noise?

MARCUS BENIGNUS: It could be him.

VOICE: ...*foffa suffesta*...

ALFREDO: I hear it, too.

GAIUS LUCIUS: *(Pointing at a broken wine cask:)*
It's coming from there.

MARCUS BENIGNUS: It could be him.

(GAIUS LUCIUS peers into the cask.)

ALFREDO: Gaius Lucius?

GAIUS LUCIUS: No, it's a Visigoth maiden.

ALFREDO: Maybe she knows where he went.

GAIUS LUCIUS: *(Reaching into the cask:)* Come here, you.
Agh! She bit me.

ALFREDO: Get out of the way. Let me see.

*(ALFREDO pushes GAIUS LUCIUS aside and peers into the
cask.)*

ALFREDO: Well, aren't you a pretty thing? Come here.
We won't hurt you. *(To Marcus Benignus:)* Marcus
Benignus, you know Gothic—

MARCUS BENIGNUS: No, I know *Spartan.*

ALFREDO: Gaius Lucius?

GAIUS LUCIUS: I know some dirty jokes in Trojan.
(Nudging MARCUS BENIGNUS:) Hey, how did the
Trojan know there were Greek spies at the orgy?

MARCUS BENIGNUS: Greeks came in a horse. Heard that
one.

ALFREDO: *(To the Visigoth:)* You're a pretty thing. Would
you like a pretty, pretty thing? *(He dangles the gold
crucifix in front of the opening in the cask.)* Yes. Good girl.

*(ALFREDO uses the crucifix to lure the Visigoth out of her
hiding place. Her clothes are ragged and dusty. ALFREDO*

brushes the matted hair out of her face. It is HELGA. *She grabs the crucifix and clutches it to her, babbling in Gothic.)*

HELGA: *Eflanifemnum. Saffron in a fepfer. Feffery....*

BLACKOUT

EPISODE 18

"Nothing but wild geese and red herrings. But the real
herring was about to hit the fan."

CHARACTERS

LARRY FINGERS
THE WEREWOLF
DICK PISTON
HARLEQUIN
WOLFGANG BIEDERMANN
HERBERTO HERMOSA
ALFREDO CENTAURI

HALLWAY OF AN APARTMENT BUILDING

(LARRY *comes down the hallway. He knocks at a door. The
door is opened by the* WEREWOLF! LARRY *takes out a set of
chains and manacles made of silver and offers them to the*
WEREWOLF. *The* WEREWOLF *slams the door in his face.*)

THE CHAPEL

(PISTON *wakes with a start.*)

PISTON: And that's when I knew! (*Pause, he realizes
he still doesn't know.*) Well, maybe not right at that
moment, but soon. Very soon. (*He begins reloading
his gun.*) You see—and perhaps I'm mixing my
proverbial metaphors, but—so far this case had
been nothing but wild geese and red herrings,
but the real herring was about to hit the fan...

HARLEQUIN

HARLEQUIN: LARRY AND THE WEREWOLF. Episode
Eighteen! Awooooo...

STREET CORNER

(BIEDERMANN *stomps in, followed by* HERMOSA.)

BIEDERMANN: Ya know, you think you know someone.
You spend your afterlife with him. Then this. The lies,

the deception. And they say "Dead men tell no tales."
Ha! And "Chivalry is dead." Ha! I'd like to see that too.

HERMOSA: And "The only good injun is a dead injun".

BIEDERMANN: Well, you're gonna have to show me a
good dead injun before I believe it, 'cause all I know
right now is if he's got a tongue in his head, put a fork
in it, 'cause you can't trust a man to give you the time
of day without stabbing you in the back with the whole
damn clock.

HERMOSA: Whatever that means.

BIEDERMANN: "Hey, can I haunt with you?" "Sure!
You're not a Russian spy or anything like that?"
"Noooo! Why would I be a Russian spy?" And then
next thing you know... Surprise! "Remember how I
told you I was a Hispanic hitman? Sorry. Russian spy."

HERMOSA: I never said I was Hispanic.

BIEDERMANN: *Herberto Hermosa?*

HERMOSA: When *I* tell the story that's a Filipino name.

BIEDERMANN: You never said you were Filipino.

HERMOSA: You never asked.

BIEDERMANN: Are you Filipino?

HERMOSA: Yes.

BIEDERMANN: You're not Filipino!! You're a Russian
spy!

HERMOSA: Ex-spy.

BIEDERMANN: You're ex-everything, you're dead.

HERMOSA: And I'm Byelorussian.

BIEDERMANN: Agh! It's like spending eternity with a
fucking lawyer.

HERMOSA: Hey, count your blessings that I'm not, buddy!

BIEDERMANN: I'm sorry. You're right. That was cold. I apologize.

HERMOSA: Okay.

(BIEDERMANN *gives* HERMOSA *a hug. Then...*)

BIEDERMANN: Hey! You tried to pick my pocket!

HERMOSA: Did not.

BIEDERMANN: Yes, you did!

HERMOSA: Just curious.

BIEDERMANN: I can't believe this!

HERMOSA: Whatta you got in there?

BIEDERMANN: And to think I trusted you.

HERMOSA: Just lemme see.

BIEDERMANN: No!

HERMOSA: Oh, what's the big hairy deal? ...No offense... It's not like you're the one I tried to have killed.

BIEDERMANN: No, I'm just the one who vouched for you when you said Larry murdered you, and now you're not even you.

HERMOSA: What did you want me to do? Tell you the truth?

BIEDERMANN: Yes.

HERMOSA: Would you have helped me?

BIEDERMANN: Well...

HERMOSA: Well?

BIEDERMANN: Well...

HERMOSA: Truth got your tongue?

BIEDERMANN: Okay, probably not.

HERMOSA: There ya go.

BIEDERMANN: And that makes it all right?

HERMOSA: Duh.

BIEDERMANN: *You* were haunting the wrong person, and now I can never haunt again, okay? How am I supposed to show my face in front of Piston and make him feel guilty about killing me by mistake when I just practically did the exact same thing?

HERMOSA: See, I don't remember you shooting anybody.

BIEDERMANN: I'm just as responsible as if I pulled the trigger myself. ...Except that I can't seem to pick up metal objects. Or things blessed by a priest.

HERMOSA: Ya know, Larry's not even dead. So you really didn't exactly just practically kill *anyone* by mistake.

BIEDERMANN: That's beside the point. My credibility is shot. Who's gonna believe me now?

HERMOSA: You're a ghost. Who's gonna believe you anyway?

BIEDERMANN: Well, if that ain't the pot calling the kettle cookware.

HERMOSA: All right, listen, I'm sorry. I know I've done some awful things in my time. And after my time. I've hurt people. I've hurt animals. But you gotta believe me when I say I never *ever* meant to hurt you— (*He can't keep a straight face.*) Let me try that again...

BIEDERMANN: And my prom date never meant to dump me, and my mom never meant to bottle-feed me, and Piston never meant to take one look at my rectum and bam bam bam bam bam bam bam click click click.

HERMOSA: Ya know, there's thing's about your past I don't really need to know.

BIEDERMANN: Well, then here's something about the ghost of Biedermann future that might not interest you either... From now on, I work alone.

HERMOSA: No, you don't mean...

BIEDERMANN: Yes, I do mean.

HERMOSA: No, you don't.

BIEDERMANN: I do.

HERMOSA: No.

BIEDERMANN: Get out.

HERMOSA: Aw, c'mon, Biedermann.

BIEDERMANN: You are dead to me.

HERMOSA: Wolfgang...

BIEDERMANN: I have no sidekick.

HERMOSA: No...

BIEDERMANN: You are dead to me.

HERMOSA: Okay. ...I guess I can't blame you. ...I'll go. *(He starts to go.)* But before I go I just want you to look me in the eye and tell me one thing.

(BIEDERMANN *looks him in the eye.)*

HERMOSA: Whatta you got in your pocket?

BIEDERMANN: Sheesh!

HERMOSA: 'Cause I'm real curious.

BIEDERMANN: You're incorrigible.

HERMOSA: In the worst way.

(BIEDERMANN *tosses Hermosa a gift-wrapped present.)*

BIEDERMANN: It was supposed to be for your birthday.

HERMOSA: Oh...

BIEDERMANN: Go ahead, open it before I find out you lied about being born.

(HERMOSA *opens his gift. It's a T-shirt that says...*)

HERMOSA: "Haunt, if you love Jesus." Oh, buddy...

BIEDERMANN: Yeah yeah yeah, get outta here.

(HERMOSA *wells up.*)

HERMOSA: I'm sorry.

BIEDERMANN: Makes two of us.

HERMOSA: I'm gonna miss you.

BIEDERMANN: Miss me over there.

HERMOSA: Take care.

BIEDERMANN: Take a hike.

HERMOSA: Hasta la vista.

BIEDERMANN: Hasta la hell freezes over.

HERMOSA: Goodbye.

BIEDERMANN: Good riddance.

(HERMOSA *sniffles.*)

BIEDERMANN: Get a kleenex.

(HERMOSA *exits, sniffling.*)

BIEDERMANN: GET A KLEENEX!! ...God, I hate that guy. Whoever he is.

(BIEDERMANN *goes out the other way.*)

ALFREDO'S APARTMENT

(ALFREDO *is getting ready for a hot date when* PISTON *bursts in.*)

ALFREDO: Piston.

PISTON: Centauri.

ALFREDO: So you counted the money. (*He throws down another stack of bills.*) I had to try, you know. My taxes are going to be a nightmare this year.

PISTON: I didn't come for the money.

ALFREDO: Well, then. (*He takes back the money.*)

PISTON: um... Well, that's not what I mean.

ALFREDO: Well, be clear, Piston. I'm not a mind reader. Except for once in Brussels. But that was a nude beach. What do you want?

PISTON: I want what I've wanted from the first time I laid eyes on you.

ALFREDO: Sex?

PISTON: No, answers!

ALFREDO: You want answers?

PISTON: I think I'm entitled.

ALFREDO: I've seen that movie, Piston.

PISTON: I had to try.

ALFREDO: I tire of this game, Piston.

PISTON: Good. That makes two of us.

ALFREDO: Perhaps you should give it a rest.

PISTON: Perhaps you should explain why the investigation keeps leading me back to you.

ALFREDO: Perhaps it's because you're incompetent.

PISTON: Perhaps it's because you're afraid to answer my questions.

ALFREDO: My theory is more plausible. But enough.
I will give you the answers you seek, but then you will go away and never trouble me again.

PISTON: You got a deal.

ALFREDO: This is not a deal, it's a threat. I don't want to see your face again, Piston, unless it's an open-casket ceremony.

PISTON: ...You still got a deal.

ALFREDO: May I take your coat?

PISTON: That's all right.

ALFREDO: Something to drink?

PISTON: I'm fine, thanks.

ALFREDO: Are you comfortable?

PISTON: Excruciatingly.

ALFREDO: Let us begin.

PISTON: Mister Centauri—

ALFREDO: Yes. No. I don't know. Yes. No. I told you, I don't know. The usual way. I'm not a zoologist, Mister Piston. Marcus Benignus and Gaius Lucius. He was a friend of mine, a gladiator. It means what it sounds like, you have a filthy mind. Of course I slept with him; you still have a filthy mind. I doubt that, but anything is possible. I'm not trying to be helpful, Mister Piston, I'm trying to be succinct. He stole my wife. Homosexuality is one of my hobbies, I also sculpt. Helga Hermosa. I saw her first. Two thousand years. No, two thousand people years. Yes, I did, but so did Larry Fingers. No, she's completely innocent. I'm positive. I believe I

answered that. Helga switched your bullets. To protect
the werewolf, of course. And that sounds like a
question for Mrs Hermosa. Good night, Mister Piston.
(*He straightens his tie and heads for the door.*)

PISTON: What? Why would Helga want to protect the
werewolf?

ALFREDO: I believe I answered that, Mister Piston.
Good night.

(ALFREDO *shuts the door in* PISTON's *face.*)

BLACKOUT

EPISODE 19

"Ooh. That's a good hint. Give me one more."

CHARACTERS

HARLEQUIN
DICK PISTON
HELGA HERMOSA
LARRY FINGERS
BILL BOLA
BELLA BOLA
FANTASY DICK
FANTASY CHICK
ALFREDO CENTAURI

HARLEQUIN

HARLEQUIN: LARRY AND THE WEREWOLF. Episode Nineteen! Awooooo...

HELGA'S APARTMENT

PISTON: Alfredo Centauri had given me all the answers, but I still had a lot of questions. In fact, I still had all the questions. That's when I decided to drop in on the widow Hermosa. She's always good for a laugh.

(*Enter* HELGA *from the next room.*)

HELGA: (*Startled:*) Agh! Oh, it's you, Mister Piston. I forgot you were out here. Sorry if I seem a bit distracted. (*She becomes distracted.*)

PISTON: Helga...

HELGA: (*Startled:*) Agh! Oh, it's you, Mister Piston. Thank you for coming. Perhaps you're wondering why I invited you here today.

PISTON: I wasn't invited.

HELGA: What?! Oh no! Help!

(HELGA *tries to run away.* PISTON *grabs her to try to calm her down.*)

HELGA: Help! Murder!

PISTON: I'm not trying to kill you!

(HELGA *grabs* PISTON's *pistol and points it at him.*)

HELGA: Aha! What *are* you trying to do to me?

(She slaps him.)

PISTON: Nothing!

HELGA: Oh.

(She gives him back his gun. On second thought, she snatches the gun away from him again.)

HELGA: Waitaminute, you went to an awful lot of trouble to do nothing to me. Are you sure you didn't come here to rob me? Just a little?

PISTON: Helga—

HELGA: And how did you get in here? All the doors are locked!

PISTON: You let me in.

HELGA: So it's an inside job! I knew it!

PISTON: I'm just going to go out and come back in again.

(PISTON goes out the front door. Pause. Knock at the door)

HELGA: *(Warily:)* Who is it?

PISTON: *(Offstage:)* Dick Piston, hotel detective.

(HELGA looks through the peephole.)

HELGA: Dick Piston! *(She throws open the door, and gives him a big hug.)* I'm so glad to see you. Come in! Come in! Have a seat!

(PISTON looks around.)

PISTON: You don't have any furniture.

HELGA: Yes! Those Bola boys did such a nice job at the hotel, I let them clean my apartment, too. Isn't it lovely? Look at this... *(She touches the floor.)* That is the only fingerprint in this apartment.

PISTON: They're very thorough.

HELGA: What brings you here?

PISTON: May I have my gun?

HELGA: Is this yours? Somebody left it.

(HELGA *hands him the gun.*)

PISTON: Ms Hermosa, I have reason to believe that I'm about to uncover the identity of your husband's murderer.

HELGA: But I thought it was that awful Wolfgang Biedermann.

PISTON: No, it turns out I was mistaken.

HELGA: Oh. But you killed him.

PISTON: I know.

HELGA: I had my doubts, but when you killed him, I thought for sure he did it.

PISTON: I know.

HELGA: That means the real murderer is still out there!

PISTON: That's right.

HELGA: He could be anywhere!

PISTON: That's right.

HELGA: He could be right here in this room!

PISTON: Well, if he's here in this room, then he's one of us.

HELGA: Agh! We've got to get out of here then!!

(PISTON *stops her from fleeing the apartment.*)

PISTON: Ms Hermosa, I'd like to ask you a few questions.

HELGA: Easy ones, I hope.

PISTON: I've been talking to Alfredo Centauri.

HELGA: True! False! Oh, I don't know. True!

PISTON: um...it's true.

HELGA: Yes!!!! One. That's one.

PISTON: He seems to think that you switched the bullets in my gun.

HELGA: Switched them with what?

PISTON: Other bullets.

HELGA: Why would I do that?

PISTON: Um...that's what I was hoping you could tell me.

HELGA: And you want that in the form of a question?

PISTON: I want that in the form why did you switch the bullets?

HELGA: Hmm... I know this one....

PISTON: Let me give you a hint.

HELGA: Yes, please. The suspense is killing me.

PISTON: Centauri says you did it to protect the Werewolf.

HELGA: Ooh. That's a good hint. Give me one more.

PISTON: Ms Hermosa, do you know who the werewolf is?

HELGA: *(Very excited:)* Who?! Who?!?!

PISTON: Maybe I should approach this another way.

HELGA: Good idea. Do you need me to move?

PISTON: When we first met, you told me you had a lover.

HELGA: True!

PISTON: This one's multiple choice.

HELGA: Ugh. Math.

PISTON: Were you referring to...?

(HELGA *listens very carefully.*)

PISTON: A: Me. Dick Piston, hotel detective.

(HELGA *shakes her head.*)

PISTON: B: Larry Fingers

HELGA: *(To herself:)* Okay, so far, B.

PISTON: Or C: Alfredo Centauri

HELGA: Oh, God, no, he's my husband. The answer is B: Larry Fingers. That was too easy.

PISTON: Alfredo's your husband?

HELGA: Well, not anymore.

PISTON: But he's gay.

HELGA: Yeah, right! Gay as a flock of bunnies. He's got enough libido for ten men. And five or six women.

PISTON: So you were married to Alfredo?

HELGA: For two thousand years.

PISTON: Two thousand years!!

HELGA: Well, it seemed like two thousand years. I guess it coulda been more....

PISTON: Why did you leave him? Was he unfaithful?

HELGA: No, I left him because of the way he kissed me.

PISTON: How did he kiss you?

HELGA: Like this...

(HELGA *kisses* PISTON.)

PISTON: Uh huh. And that bothered you?

HELGA: Larry kissed me like this.

(HELGA *kisses* PISTON *again. This time,* PISTON *goes weak in the knees.*)

HELGA: I mean, is it just me, or is Larry a better kisser?

PISTON: *(Woozy:)* Show me Larry again.

(HELGA *kisses* PISTON *again...*)

LARRY'S STUDIO

(As LARRY *glares at* BELLA, *he plays a macabre piano piece.* BILL *stands off to one side, fidgeting nervously.)*

BELLA: Well, what did you want me to do? Let him keep shooting till you caught a stray bullet? I had to say something. Don't let that kevlar vest go to your head, Larry. You're not made of kryptonite. One of these days, somebody's gonna aim a little high and you'll be wiping that smirk off the upholstery.

BILL: Bella...

BELLA: I don't care, Bill, this is bullshit. *(To* LARRY:*)* We saved your life at that wedding, and you know it. *And* we got you that nice crockpot. And this is the thanks we get?

BILL: Bella...

BELLA: No, Bill, I want him to say it. *(To* LARRY:*)* Say it!!

(LARRY *says nothing.*)

BELLA: Okay, I get it. Larry Fingers doesn't need our help. Larry Fingers doesn't need anybody. I guess it must be Santa Claus slipping instructions under my door in sealed envelopes every morning.

BILL: ...Santa?

BELLA: Well, if you see Santa, tell him here's the silver bullets he asked for. Here's the dossier on Piston. Here's the wiretap for Helga's apartment. And here's my letter of resignation.

(LARRY *stops playing.*)

BILL: *(Whispers:)* And I wanna bike.

BELLA: That's right, me and Bill, we're going straight. And don't try to talk us out of it. We'll temp for the C I A until we can find honest work. I hear the A T F is hiring. They've got a great benefits package and you still get to kill people.

(LARRY starts playing again.)

BELLA: Yeah, okay, I don't know why I thought you'd care. Let's get outta here, Bill.

(BILL gives BELLA a stern look. She turns to LARRY again.)

BELLA: Larry...I never thanked you for helping us out with the K G B. I probably coulda outrun the Soviet death squads. But Bill... Well, Bill owes you his life.

BILL: Thanks, Larry.

BELLA: And I'll always be grateful for that.

(LARRY just keeps playing.)

BELLA: You may be the world's biggest asshole, Larry. But I'm glad I met you.

(LARRY takes out a gun and shoots BILL dead. BELLA looks at Bill, looks at LARRY.)

BELLA: You may be the world's biggest asshole, Larry.

FANTASY

(FANTASY DICK and the FANTASY CHICK study the mysterious note.)

FANTASY CHICK: It must be from him. The man who's been following me.

FANTASY DICK: But why would he use my handwriting? And whose blood is this?

FANTASY CHICK: It's his blood.

FANTASY DICK: You've never seen this man's face, but you recognize his blood?

FANTASY CHICK: No, I just happen to know that he's bleeding.

FANTASY DICK: Is he a hemophiliac?

FANTASY CHICK: Yes, if that's Latin for gunshot victim.

FANTASY DICK: You shot him?

FANTASY CHICK: Just once. With this.

(*She shows him a pearl-handled revolver.*)

FANTASY DICK: Why, this wouldn't kill a fly.

FANTASY CHICK: I wasn't trying to kill him. I love him.

FANTASY DICK: Love him?

FANTASY CHICK: Yes. He makes me feel hunted. Wanted. Feminine. That's why I need you to find him.

(FANTASY DICK *removes his jacket. He is bleeding from a gunshot wound in his shoulder.*)

FANTASY DICK: It's me.

HELGA'S APARTMENT

(*A trail of* PISTON's *clothing leads off into* HELGA's *bedroom. Their voices can be heard.*)

PISTON: (*Offstage:*) Helga!

HELGA: (*Offstage:*) Larry!

PISTON: (*Offstage:*) Dick.

HELGA: (*Offstage:*) Larry!

PISTON: (*Offstage:*) Dick, Helga, Dick!

(*The front door opens.* ALFREDO *enters with a bouquet of flowers and a box of chocolates.*)

HELGA: *(Offstage:)* Yes!

PISTON: *(Offstage:)* Yes!

HELGA: *(Offstage:)* Yes!

PISTON: *(Offstage:)* Yes!

(ALFREDO *crosses to the bedroom door and peers in.*
He lets out a growl as he drops the flowers, and charges
into the bedroom.)

PISTON: *(Offstage:)* YES! YES! YES! YES! NO! OH, NO!
OH, NO!

(*Animal snarls and rending sounds.* PISTON *is flung*
backward into the room.)

PISTON: Helga! No!

BLACKOUT

EPISODE 20

"Multiple gunshot wounds won't keep a good man down."

CHARACTERS

HARLEQUIN
ALFREDO CENTAURI
MARCUS BENIGNUS
GAIUS LUCIUS
HELGA HERMOSA
WOLFGANG BIEDERMANN
SPIKE
LARRY FINGERS
DICK PISTON

HARLEQUIN

HARLEQUIN: LARRY AND THE WEREWOLF. Episode Twenty! Awooooo...

ROME—TWELVE B.C.

(HELGA *and the three* CENTURIONS *are sitting around a campfire.* HELGA *plays with her crucifix.* ALFREDO *watches, enthralled. The other* CENTURIONS *watch, enraged.)*

ALFREDO: Look at her. She's beautiful. Angelic. Radiant.

MARCUS BENIGNUS: She's a dirty little Visigoth.

ALFREDO: *(Grabbing him by the throat:)* You take that back.

MARCUS BENIGNUS: Go ahead, rip my heart out. It won't be the first time.

GAIUS LUCIUS: Leave him alone, Marcus Benignus. The Centurion's never been with a woman.

ALFREDO: I've been with a woman.

GAIUS LUCIUS: Oh, I see. Then it's just that you have no taste.

ALFREDO: No, Gaius Lucius, it's just that my tastes are diverse. And yours are strictly perverse.

GAIUS LUCIUS: At least I know what I want.

ALFREDO: I know what I want! *(Gazing at* HELGA*)* I want this moment to last forever. This burning. This feeling. This... love.

MARCUS BENIGNUS: Love? But... But... But what about "us"?

GAIUS LUCIUS: That's it, Marcus Benignus, whine and babble. The Centurion likes that in a woman.

ALFREDO: *(To* GAIUS LUCIUS*:)* Give me your ring.

GAIUS LUCIUS: What? Why?

ALFREDO: I'm going to marry her.

GAIUS LUCIUS: You gave me this ring.

ALFREDO: I am reclaiming it. I grow tired of you.

*(*GAIUS LUCIUS *glares at* ALFREDO *as he removes his ring and hands it to him.)*

GAIUS LUCIUS: You shall grow tireder.

ALFREDO: Marcus Benignus. Give me yours.

MARCUS BENIGNUS: *(Clutching his ring:)* But Centurion—

*(*ALFREDO *draws his sword and points it at* MARCUS BENIGNUS*'s throat.)*

ALFREDO: Don't make me reason with you.

MARCUS BENIGNUS: I refuse.

*(*ALFREDO *chops off* MARCUS BENIGNUS*'s finger and takes the ring.* MARCUS BENIGNUS *screams and clutches his hand.)*

ALFREDO: You two shall be my witnesses.

*(*GAIUS LUCIUS *walks out.)*

ALFREDO: *(To* HELGA*:)* My angel?

*(*HELGA *looks at him.* ALFREDO *shows her the two rings. He puts one on her hand, and then puts the other on his own hand.)*

ALFREDO: *(Pointing at* HELGA*, then himself:)* You... are *mine.*

HELGA: *(Pointing at herself:)* Helga.

ALFREDO: *(Pointing at* HELGA, *then himself:)* Helga...
is mine.

HELGA: *(Pointing at herself, then* ALFREDO:*)* Helga.
...Mine.

MARCUS BENIGNUS: *(Bitterly:)* How romantic.

ALFREDO: *(Picking* MARCUS BENIGNUS *up by the throat:)*
Roman bitch!

MARCUS BENIGNUS: *(Being strangled:)* The hand!
The hand!

(While they are fighting, and HELGA *is admiring her
new ring,* GAIUS LUCIUS *walks back in as a werewolf.
He crosses to* HELGA, *and sinks his teeth into her throat.
She is dead before* ALFREDO *can even react.)*

ALFREDO: No!!

*(*GAIUS LUCIUS *ignores him and calmly sits down next to the
body.)*

GAIUS LUCIUS: Now, let's see what happens.

BIEDERMANN

*(*BIEDERMANN *climbs onto a chair and puts a noose around
his neck.)*

BIEDERMANN: Ya know how to pinpoint the moment of
death? It's not when the heart stops pumping. Or the
lungs. Or activity in the brain. It's when you lose the
will to live. That's how you know. Multiple gunshot
wounds can't keep a good man down. But when you
wake up in the morning and ask yourself, "Why am
I here?" and the answer comes back, "No special
reason." Then it's over. The bullets can come before.
After. It doesn't matter. People die and go on living all

the time. You really wanna kill someone, you gotta rip their world apart. Shatter their illusions. Take away the things they believe in. Or be one of those things. And betray them. ...Yeah. ...That's how ya do it. (*He steps off the chair. The rope jerks taut. He twitches briefly, then goes limp. Silence. He opens his eyes.*) Well, somebody get me down from here.

LARRY FINGERS AND SPIKE

(*Lights up on* LARRY *and* SPIKE *in concert.* SPIKE *is dressed in extravagant mourning garb. She sings psychotically.*)

SPIKE: How you gonna live without me, now that you said goodbye?
How you gonna look another mirror in the eye?
How you gonna even sleep nights in that big half-empty bed?
How you gonna live without me...?

Somewhere there is joy in Mudville.
Somewhere children shout.
Somewhere there is joy in Mudville...

Where you gonna turn for comfort when you need a hand to hold?
And I'm not there to tell you when to come in from the cold?
Or walk along beside you down the lonely road ahead?
How you gonna live without me...?

Somewhere there is joy in Mudville.
Somewhere children shout.
Somewhere there is joy in Mudville...

YOU CUT OFF YOUR OWN DAMN LEGS,
SO DON'T COME RUNNING TO ME!
THAT BRIDGE IS BURNED, YOU CAN'T RETURN
UNLESS YOU'RE GONNA PART THE SEA!

I HAVE TURNED THE OTHER CHEEK,
BUT YOU JUST TURN YOUR BACK!
IF JESUS CHRIST WERE HERE RIGHT NOW,
HE'D TELL YOU TO GO FUCK YOURSELF!!

Billie was a girl on the ropes.
Couldn't cope with the dope.
She knew there wasn't much hope...
Until she met the Pope.

Hey, Billie! said the Pope, you lookin' cute in that dress,
with your high heel shoes, and your black lace panties,
won't you come over here and baby give us a smile,
sit on my lap or maybe dinner tonight maybe drinks
and go drivin' in my '57 Chevy with the top down
wind in my face, feel the blood racin' like a (Ooh), like a
(Ah), white hot , like a animal, pawing you, caressing
and gnawing you, molesting and—NO, POPE, NO!!

(While LARRY *launches into a piano solo,* SPIKE *comes
downstage for a moment with the audience.)*

SPIKE: You been a great audience. Thank you. Even the
ones who couldn't be here tonight. Our fans, I mean.
We couldn't have done it without you. Except the ones
who couldn't be here tonight. I guess we did it without
you. But whether you're here tonight or not... You were
always there for us... And now here we are. *(She glances
at* LARRY.*)* Wherever that is... *(Upbeat:)* And you're here
too! ...some of you... So this is great! It's like one
big...something.

*(*SPIKE *watches* LARRY *improvise.)*

SPIKE: This doesn't have an ending. This song.
Unless that was it and it's already over. I guess I gotta
stop thinkin' every story has to have a silver lining.
Sometimes they're just stories. One more thing, I guess
I should tell you. Because of recent...personal... Because
of artistic differences, this will be our last public
performance.

(Sings How you gonna live without me, after all that
   we been through?
And every little everything I've ever done for you
How you gonna take back all the words we left unsaid?
How you gonna live without me...? Wouldn't you be
   better off dead?

*(SPIKE takes a gun out of her bodice and turns to shoot
LARRY.)*

SPIKE: I love you, Larry.

(Just then, PISTON springs up behind LARRY, with a gun.)

PISTON: Then you're gonna love this.

(He takes LARRY hostage.)

SPIKE: Wait! I'm the one you want!

PISTON: You are?

(Long pause. It's hard for her to admit.)

SPIKE: ...No, I'm not. I tried, Larry, I tried!

PISTON: Let's go, Larry. We're gonna have a little talk.

*(PISTON drags LARRY offstage at gunpoint, as SPIKE stands
helplessly by. HARLEQUIN enters.)*

HARLEQUIN: I wish I could take a hostage. Twist a plot.
I wish I had a gun. And a guitar. And a way with
women. Something more substantial than
imagination...and paper.

*(HARLEQUIN holds up a blank sheet of paper. He drops it in
front of SPIKE. She picks it up.)*

SPIKE: A ransom note! *(Reads:)* "If you hope to see Larry
alive, meet me at the hospital." *(She dashes out.)*

HARLEQUIN: *(To the audience:)* If you hope to see Larry
die, meet me in the next episode. Awooooo...

BLACKOUT

EPISODE 21

"You don't frighten us, Piston, with your gun and your truth."

CHARACTERS

DICK PISTON
HARLEQUIN
LARRY FINGERS
SPIKE
HELGA HERMOSA
ALFREDO CENTAURI
MARCUS BENIGNUS
BILL BOLA
BELLA BOLA
THE SPANISH GHOST
THIRD CENTURION
FANTASY DICK
FANTASY CHICK

PISTON

PISTON: I thought for sure Wolfgang Biedermann was the werewolf. Until I shot him. Then I found out Larry Fingers was the werewolf. I was sure about that, too. So I shot him. Then I saw a ghost, had a dream, and ran into a werewolf of my own. Now, all I know for sure, is every time I know for sure, an innocent bystander takes a bullet. "Perhaps it's because you're incompetent," Alfredo Centauri might say. And by "you" he'd mean me, Dick Piston, hotel detective. Maybe he's right. Maybe I'm outta my proverbial league, my proverbial element, my proverbial mind thinking I can catch this guy. Maybe instead of chasing the killer, I should just cut out the middle man and go after innocent bystanders directly. *(He starts to reload his gun.)* So I kidnapped Larry Fingers. The story he told me you're not gonna believe...

HARLEQUIN

(Enter HARLEQUIN, *dressed for the finale.)*

HARLEQUIN: LARRY AND THE WEREWOLF. Episode Twenty-One!

*(*HARLEQUIN *transforms the stage into a hospital room around* PISTON.*)*

HOSPITAL ROOM

(ALFREDO *lies in the hospital bed, in traction.* MARCUS BENIGNUS *is at his bedside, holding his hand.* HELGA *sits in a motorized wheelchair with bandages over her eyes.* LARRY *is tied to a chair with duct tape over his mouth.* SPIKE *rushes in.)*

SPIKE: Larry!! *(To* PISTON:*)* Piston, what have you done??

PISTON: I tied him to a chair.

SPIKE: And taped his mouth shut! You monster!! Larry's a poet. Shutting his mouth is like death to him. It would be like if someone cut off your...your... *(She looks him up and down.)* Your gun, I guess.

PISTON: Don't worry, Spike. Larry's said his proverbial piece.

SPIKE: Larry? What did you tell him?

PISTON: Oh, Larry sang like a canary, Spike. Larry squealed like a proverbial pig.

SPIKE: *(To* PISTON:*)* You didn't!!

PISTON: Um... no, I didn't. Allow me to retract the pig metaphor.

SPIKE: Good. *(Hugging* LARRY:*)* I don't think I could stand another betrayal.

PISTON: I believe you've met my other guests. Helga Hermosa.

HELGA: Hi!

PISTON: And Alfredo Centauri.

HELGA: What? Alfredo's here?! Oh no! *(She makes a run for it in her motorized wheelchair.)*

PISTON: Not so fast, Helga.

(HELGA *stops. Then she makes a run for it slowly in her motorized wheelchair.*)

PISTON: Helga!

(HELGA *stops. She pouts.*)

SPIKE: (*Noticing* HELGA'*s bandaged face:*) What is this, Piston, some sort of clandestine organ harvesting operation?

PISTON: No, it's a hospital.

SPIKE: Oh. (*She looks at* HELGA, *looks at* PISTON.) 'Cause I could use an eye.

PISTON: I'm not harvesting organs!

SPIKE: Just asking.

PISTON: The hospital seemed like a convenient meeting place since Alfredo and Helga were here already. They had a little run in with a werewolf.

HELGA: What? Alfredo's here?!

(HELGA *makes a run for it in her motorized wheelchair.* PISTON *disconnects her battery.* HELGA'*s wheelchair stops, but she still thinks she's going.*)

HELGA: Vrrrrrrrr...

SPIKE: A werewolf? Then that crazy story isn't just some cockamamie story you came up with to sell tickets?

PISTON: No, Spike, the werewolf is as real as you or I.

SPIKE: Well, who is it?

PISTON: Not just yet. I'm expecting two more guests.

(*Enter* BELLA, *pushing* BILL *in a wheelchair.*)

PISTON: Belladonna Bola, and her brother.

BELLA: Sorry I'm late. I woulda been here sooner, but you told me to bring Bill with me.

PISTON: He doesn't look well.

BELLA: He's as healthy as a horse.

SPIKE: A dead horse.

PISTON: Dead?

BELLA: Yeah, I thought you knew that.

PISTON: Oh my God. I didn't know he was dead.

BELLA: Take it or leave it, Piston.

PISTON: Oh my God, I didn't know. I wouldn't have asked you to bring him, if I'd known. Oh my God. I'm so sorry.

BELLA: What? I was up all night digging, and you don't need him?

PISTON: Oh my God.

BELLA: You're starting to grate on me, Piston.

(HELGA *leaps out of her wheelchair.*)

HELGA: Now, I'll ditch the wheelchair in this alley and make my getaway on foot.

PISTON: Helga!

HELGA: Mister Piston! I should have known you'd find me.

PISTON: Sit!

(HELGA *sits, pouts.*)

PISTON: Thank you all for coming. For those of you just joining us—last night I did something I should've done a long time ago.

ALFREDO: Got a life?

(*Everybody has a little laugh at* PISTON'*s expense.*)

PISTON: I got the truth out of Larry Fingers.

BELLA: I didn't think he had it in him.

(PISTON *holds up a cassette tape.*)

PISTON: On this tape is enough information to put all of you away for a very long time. Ladies and gentlemen, the confession of Larry Fingers...

(PISTON *plays the tape. It is blank.*)

PISTON: What the...???

(*Even with his mouth taped,* LARRY *seems to be snickering.*)

EVERYBODY: Well, this has been fun, gotta go, gotta get up early tomorrow...

PISTON: I may not have the tape, but I still know the truth. And I've still got the gun.

MARCUS BENIGNUS: You don't frighten us, Piston, with your gun and your truth.

PISTON: And my silver bullets?

MARCUS BENIGNUS: Oh shit! Oh shit! Silver bullets, Alfredo!

ALFREDO: Silence!

HELGA: *(Waving:)* Hi, Marcus!

ALFREDO: Go on, Mister Piston.

HELGA: Can we at least go back to the hospital? This alley stinks.

(PISTON *takes out the silver chains, and throws them down.*)

HELGA: Marley?

SPIKE: Where did you get those?

PISTON: From your bedroom, Spike. They're chains. Silver chains. Chains strong enough to hold a werewolf. Larry told me he uses them during sex.

SPIKE: No, *those are just for show*. We get by with duct tape and a little twine.

PISTON: Well, somebody's been using them. I had these chains examined by a police cosmetologist who found animal hairs in the manacles, traces of mousse and a ton of hair spray. That tells me two things. Werewolf. Big date.

SPIKE: But it's not me. I wouldn't hurt a flea. The leather collars and spikes are just for show.

PISTON: And the vice record? And the double homicide in Wisconsin. Are those just for show?

SPIKE: Larry, you told him about Wisconsin?

PISTON: Larry told me about everything! ...Well, unless there's more.

SPIKE: No, that's it. I killed two men in Milwaukee. And then I became a prostitute. But they had it coming!

PISTON: The two men? Or the other men?

SPIKE: It was justifiable homicide. They tried to force me to have sex with them. And their monkey. After I killed them, I had to turn to prostitution to pay my legal fees. Which were enormous because even though it was self defense, I didn't have an airtight alibi like a rich husband or a pro football career...

PISTON: *(To audience:)* You're probably wondering why I let her go on like that. Well, you see it's to illustrate a point. Evil, like time, is relative. On a scale of one to ten, Spike Snodgrass, prostitute and double murderer was maybe a one. And a perfect ten would be something like... Larry Fingers.

SPIKE: ...so when Larry blackmailed the warden into planning my escape, of course I agreed to be in his band, but then—

PISTON: All right, Spike, I believe you. But Larry Fingers was doing the proverbial nasty with *someone* hairy and lupine. Wasn't he, Alfredo?

ALFREDO: All right. I am the werewolf! Is that what you want to hear, Mister Piston? Two thousand years ago, I was a Roman Centurion in charge of three legions patrolling near Rome, I was attacked by a werewolf, and infected with its disease. I killed Herberto Hermosa because he stole my wife from me. But I defy you to prove it.

PISTON: I don't intend to prove it. Because it's not true. Herberto Hermosa didn't steal your wife from you. He stole her from Larry Fingers. Who stole her from you. If jealousy were your motive, shouldn't Larry be dead, too?

ALFREDO: Don't remind me.

HELGA: *(Interrupting:)* Poppycock!! ...I've always wanted to say that.... You honestly expect me to believe that I had an affair with *this* man?

(HELGA *points at* BILL. PISTON *adjusts her finger so it points at* LARRY. HELGA *giggles. Whispers:)*

HELGA: Not now, Larry.

PISTON: Helga, you *told* me you had an affair with him.

HELGA: *(To* PISTON:) Ssh! Just play along and let me do the talking. *(Aloud:)* Ha! What possible attraction could there be? He's a *musician*, for God's sake! And his penis is enormous! You think I'd throw away two thousand years of marriage for that?

PISTON: That and five milligrams of rohypnol.

BELLA & SPIKE: The date rape drug?!

(They exchange glances.)

BELLA & SPIKE: Not that I would know.

HELGA: *(Whispers:)* What's rohypnol?

PISTON: Yes, the date rape drug. *(Holding up a vial of rohypnol:)* Which Larry Fingers was manufacturing in Mexico with the help of his Hispanic henchman Herberto Hermosa and distributing in this country to unsavory characters at our nation's high schools, night clubs and Kennedy family functions. But I digress. Because the question we should be asking Helga Hermosa is not "Why did she leave Alfredo Centauri?" but "Why did she *stay* with Larry Fingers?"

HELGA: Why did she?

PISTON: Would you like to answer that, Alfredo?

ALFREDO: Because Larry Fingers is a sadistic manipulative—

PISTON: Nope.

ALFREDO: Because Larry Fingers is a diabolically corrupt—

PISTON: Nope.

ALFREDO: Because—

PISTON: Nope.

ALFREDO: Well, it can't be the penis, I'm a Roman Centurion, for God's sake.

PISTON: Because Larry gave her something no man had ever given her before.

ALFREDO: What?

HELGA: I'd rather not say.

(Pause. Then SPIKE *and* BELLA *both gasp.)*

PISTON: She left you because you could not give her the one thing that Larry Fingers—and every man since— *has* given her.

HELGA: *(Blushing:)* Mister Piston!

MARCUS BENIGNUS: Oh my.

ALFREDO: What?!? What!?!

PISTON: But I digress. Because the part of your unsolicited confession that really doesn't hold proverbial water, Alfredo, is that after you were attacked two thousand years ago and infected with a disease which turned you into a werewolf whenever you became aroused, irate, or otherwise emotionally available, you sequestered yourself in a Buddhist monastery where they taught you to suppress your emotions. You haven't been a werewolf in hundreds of years. So you couldn't have been a werewolf on the night of the murder.

ALFREDO: Very clever, Mister Piston. But how do you know about the monastery? That is a secret shared only by myself, Marcus Benignus, Helga, Gaius Lucius, all the monks... *(He gasps.)* ...and the Beatles.

PISTON: That's right, those lovable moptops. *(Holding up a copy of the* Magical Mystery Tour *and pointing at a figure on the cover:)* Who, in 1967, had just welcomed young Larry Fingers into their fab foursome after the tragic death of Paul, who was later replaced with a talentless look-alike when it was discovered that Larry had planned the assassination in the first place. But that's a story for another time. Larry first met you at Rishikesh when you stopped in for a Zen tune-up. He also met your travelling companions. Helga, a Visigoth maiden. And another Roman Centurion-turned-werewolf... *(Accusingly:)* Marcus Benignus!

MARCUS BENIGNUS: If those weren't silver bullets, I'd kill you where you stand.

ALFREDO: Marcus...

MARCUS BENIGNUS: *(To* PISTON:*)* Never mind.

PISTON: Well, I guess we see who wears the leash in this family. *(To* MARCUS BENIGNUS*:)* He says "Bark" and you say "How high?" He says "Kill" and you say "Grrrrr. Rrarrgh. Woof woof! Rarrr..."

MARCUS BENIGNUS: Your accent is lousy.

ALFREDO: I did not tell him to murder Hermosa.

PISTON: No, but you told him to murder me. *(To* MARCUS BENIGNUS*:)* You're the werewolf who mugged me in the burning hotel.

ALFREDO: Ha! I sent him to *save* you. I told Marcus that there was a fire at the hotel and you should be informed.

MARCUS BENIGNUS: Oh. um...I thought...I thought you said...chloroformed.

(Pause)

ALFREDO: *(Furious:)* And what about Herberto Hermosa? I told you he should be followed. Did you think I said swallowed???

MARCUS BENIGNUS: No, Alfredo. Believe me. I did not swallow him.

PISTON: No, he didn't. You see, the man who murdered Herberto Hermosa was... *(Pause)* Helga Hermosa!

HELGA: I won! I won! Waitaminute....

ALFREDO: That's ridiculous. Why would she kill her own husband?

PISTON: She wouldn't, of course. *Or would she*? No, no, she wouldn't. *Or would she*? Nah, probably not. *Or would she?*

ALFREDO: Well, which is it, dammit?!?!

MARCUS BENIGNUS: Alfredus...

ALFREDO *(Calming himself:)* ...One messy poppy, two messy poppy, three messy poppy...

PISTON: It isn't easy keeping the wolf at bay, is it?

ALFREDO: You have no idea.

PISTON: Ever try to quit smoking?

ALFREDO: Oh. Well, then you know.

PISTON: Even after two thousand years it's a constant struggle. A struggle Marcus Benignus loses on weeknights at eleven.

MARCUS BENIGNUS: Jerry Springer. Grr...

PISTON: ...And then there's Helga.

HELGA: Hi!

PISTON: Who only loses control when sexually aroused.

HELGA: I'm not buying any of this.

PISTON: Fortunately she was married to you, Alfredo.

ALFREDO: One messy poppy, two messy poppy...

PISTON: But after she left you, things got a little hairy— pardon the proverbial pun. Not at first, because Larry Fingers practices safe sex. Helga was always chained to the bed when they made love, or a radiator.

SPIKE: (Sobs:) How romantic.

PISTON: But her next lover, Herberto Hermosa was not so careful. And a latex condom while generally effective in combination with a good spermicide, just won't keep out a werewolf.

HELGA: So, I'm the murderer?

BELLA: Duh.

HELGA: But I was with Larry. Tell them, Larry. ...Larry?

PISTON: You may have been fantasizing about Larry Fingers. But wherever your mind was, your body was with Herberto Hermosa. Ripping his body to shreds.

HELGA: I don't remember any of this.

PISTON: No, Helga, you don't. After being raised by Visigoths, attacked by a werewolf, forced into a loveless marriage with a pan-sexual Roman Centurion who dragged you across Asia for centuries until you were seduced away by a musician, then a matador, your fragile psyche is barely fit to remember your own name, let alone the details of a bizarre murder committed during a fit of sexual frenzy.

(Pause)

HELGA: Who are you talking to?

BELLA: Piston?

PISTON: Yes?

BELLA: Why am I here?

PISTON: um... I guess I didn't need you.

BELLA: Rrgh.

HELGA: What are you going to do to me?

PISTON: Nothing, Helga. The ghost of Herberto Hermosa forgave you. I don't see why society can't do the same. You may be a homicidal werebeast, but there are worse monsters in the world. There are worse monsters in this room. Incestuous Israeli assassins. The vengeful Zen Roman cuckold and his lycanthropic sycophant. Spike Snodgrass the O J Simpson of dominatrix lounge singers. And let's not forget me, Dick Piston, hotel vigilante. Where can we pin the proverbial blame— *(Everybody points at someone.)* —in the case of a supernatural killer whose occult evil pales in comparison to the evil of a single man? And by that, I mean, the evil of one man, not the evil of unmarried men in general. And that one man is Larry Fingers— mild-mannered pianist and sadistic necrophile, double agent, cannibal, Mafia kingpin, and anti-Semitic terrorist pimp.

(LARRY *leaps up out of his chair and steals* PISTON'S *gun.*)

PISTON: Oh, and I forgot to mention escape artist.

(LARRY *holds them all at gunpoint.*)

SPIKE: Larry, don't do it!

BELLA: Larry, widen your stance!

PISTON: You can't win. What are you going to do, Larry?

(LARRY *points the gun at* PISTON.)

PISTON: Okay. You win.

(LARRY *smiles maliciously. Then, after a tense moment, he lowers the weapon. ...and shoots* HELGA.)

PISTON: No!

(ALFREDO *leaps out of bed with a bellow of rage and slams* LARRY *into the wall.* PISTON *tries to intervene, but ends up pinned behind* LARRY, *gasping for breath.* ALFREDO *holds* LARRY *by both arms and sinks his teeth into* LARRY'S *neck. While* LARRY *gurgles in pain,* PISTON *manages to get the gun out of his hand, and shoots* ALFREDO *in the chest. Twice.* ALFREDO *dies.* LARRY *dies, too. And the* SPANISH GHOST *materializes in the room.*)

SPANISH GHOST: Good work, Piston.

(*Everything is silent in the stunned aftermath of the battle until* HELGA *blurts...*)

HELGA: Is it just me, or is anyone else floating out of their body?

(*The* SPANISH GHOST *takes* HELGA *by the hand and helps her up from her wheelchair. Removing the bandages from her eyes, he takes her in his arms and kisses her, as the lights begin to fade...*)

EPILOGUE

(*...to an isolated spot on* HARLEQUIN *standing over the body of* LARRY.)

HARLEQUIN: So the ghost gets the girl. The devil gets his due. And the dog has his day in court. Don't you wish. Justice is balance. But Life is chaos. Justice is poetic. Reality is utterly without rhyme or rhythm.

(LARRY *begins to stir.*)

HARLEQUIN: The Centurion's revenge on the man who gave his wife pleasure is to infect him with immortality? Where's the symmetry in that? (*Shrugs:*) When in Rome...

(HARLEQUIN *gestures and the sky darkens and it begins to rain.*)

A WINDSWEPT HILLSIDE OUTSIDE ROME

HARLEQUIN: Justice is a poem. A work of fiction. But aren't we all?

(LARRY *rises painfully to his feet.*)

HARLEQUIN: (*To* LARRY:) Welcome to Rome.

(*He disappears into the shadows, leaving* LARRY *alone on a windswept mountainside.* LARRY *howls. Then he tears off his shirt and his gold crucifix, and lopes off down the hill. Just then the* THIRD CENTURION *enters. He picks up the crucifix and holds it up. Lightning flashes. And he is gone.*)

VOICES IN THE DARKNESS

FANTASY CHICK: *(In the darkness:)* Dick... Piston...

FANTASY DICK: *(In the darkness:)* I don't wanna hear it.

(Lights up on FANTASY DICK and the FANTASY CHICK.)

FANTASY DICK: You hired me to find me knowing that I could never admit to being the man I was. It's all a game to you, isn't it?

FANTASY CHICK: You knew how to end it.

FANTASY DICK: We both did. *(Moment of sexual tension.)* So why didn't we?

FANTASY CHICK: Because, Dick. It's not whether you win or lose.

FANTASY DICK: It's how you play.

(She smiles seductively.)

FANTASY CHICK: Game over.

FANTASY DICK: There's still one thing that bothers me...

(She strips off her robe.)

FANTASY CHICK: ...I hope that was it.

FANTASY DICK: Not at all.

(He sweeps her into his arms. Just then, PISTON enters.)

PISTON: There's still one thing that bothers me...

FANTASY DICK: Not a good time, Dick.

PISTON: *(To FANTASY CHICK:)* When I was dying, you told me you were real.

FANTASY CHICK: Is that what I said?

PISTON: What *did* you say? I thought I'd find you if I solved this case. Where are you?

FANTASY CHICK: I'm a fantasy, Dick. Where do you want me?

(Moment of sexual tension.)

PISTON: That's not an answer!

(She turns with a coy laugh and slinks away. Piston watches her depart, as the lights begin to fade very slowly, and HARLEQUIN *appears out of the shadows.)*

HARLEQUIN: *(Whispers:)* You'll find her in the sequel.

PISTON: Sequel?

HARLEQUIN: *(Pointing at* PISTON's *notepad:)* The one where you die...

BLACKOUT

END OF PLAY